Praise for The Self-Led Educator

• • •

"*The Self-Led Educator* offers a clear road map for educators to cultivate calm, compassionate, and confident learning communities by fostering Self-leadership in themselves and their students. Learn practical strategies to navigate daily challenges, understand inner dynamics, and create a truly supportive and thriving learning environment."

—**Gabrielle Bernstein,** #1 *New York Times* best-selling author

"I am so impressed with this book that I plan to recommend it to anyone who wants a clear model for how IFS can be applied outside of psychotherapy. We have ambitions to expand IFS and Self-leadership beyond the limits of psychotherapy to areas like medicine, social activism, business and political leadership, and more, and this book is a great template for that expansion."

—**Richard Schwartz, PhD,** founder of Internal Family Systems Therapy

"Wow! *The Self-Led Educator* is a must-read for all educators. It shows how to have good working relationships with students, parents, and members of the community. Its deep insights have the power to transform the atmosphere of classrooms, so that students engage with their lessons more effectively while also developing and nurturing the positive aspects of their character. Joanna's book has the power to change lives, as it helps both educators and students to flourish!"

—**Dr. Neil Hawkes,** global advocate for ethical leadership and founder of Values-based Education (VbE) and the IVET Foundation

"Joanna takes the deep and powerful tools of IFS and makes them simple, memorable—even fun! If every school adopted her approach, we'd unlock a kinder, calmer, and profoundly healthier society."

—**Evan Sharp,** co-founder of Pinterest

"My years as an educator of health professionals, teachers, and athletes showed me that facts are not enough to perform well in the real world. Emotional skills are essential and now can be easily acquired. In *The Self-Led Educator*, Joanna Curry-Sartori applies the scientific and user-friendly approach of Internal

Family Systems (IFS) to fill serious gaps in current personal skill training for educators, including how to put the metaphorical oxygen mask on yourself before trying to teach others. Using her practical PAUSE model offers welcome relief from the shame-based approach experienced for years by educators, children, and parents."

—**John B. Livingstone, MD, FRSH,** child psychiatrist, member of the Harvard Medical School Academy of Medical Education, and co-author of *Relationship Power in Health Care: Science of Behavior Change, Decision Making, and Clinician Self-Care*

"*The Self-Led Educator* is a compelling resource for anyone working with children; Joanna Curry-Sartori has created a gift for the reader. She navigates the educator through the process of personally actualizing the PAUSE process through descriptions, examples, and practice and then applying it with students. This is a must-have book for educators seeking to nurture well-being, connections, collaboration, and caring that begins from within. Having experience with the power of the PAUSE model, I highly recommend *The Self-Led Educator*."

—**Karen L. List, PhD,** retired superintendent of schools; founder and project director of the PK-3 Leadership Program at the University of Connecticut's Neag School of Education

"If you care about the adults who care about kids, buy this book—and give a copy to every teacher you know. Joanna Curry-Sartori has put in the work, both personally and professionally, and it shows. *The Self-Led Educator* is well-written and researched and is based on extensive global experience. It is both practical and inspirational. The author has stayed focused on her mission to bring Self-leadership to schools so that all humans in schools can show up as their best selves. Reading *The Self-Led Educator* gave me a sense of hope that it is possible!"

—**Jody Nelson, EdD, LMFT,** senior director of the Change Institute in Minnesota, which provides school-based mental health services in six school districts

THE SELF-LED EDUCATOR

AN IFS-INSPIRED GUIDE

to Create Calm, Compassionate &
Confident Learning Communities

JOANNA CURRY-SARTORI, LMFT

THE SELF-LED EDUCATOR

Published by
PESI Publishing, Inc.
3839 White Ave
Eau Claire, WI 54703

Cover design by Lisa Kerans
Interior design by Emily Dyer
Editing by Chelsea Thompson

ISBN 9781683738589 (print)
ISBN 9781683738596 (ePUB)
ISBN 9781683738602 (ePDF)

Printed in the United States of America.

The tools offered in this book are not intended to replace therapeutic treatment with a trained professional. If you experience a strong emotional response or wish to deepen your individual exploration, you are encouraged to find a trained IFS therapist.

• • •

This book is dedicated in honor of my parents, Margaret Ennis and Steve Curry, and my stepparents, Michael Ennis and Carol Groneman. Each of you has lived a life dedicated to continual learning—pursuing your own growth while creating welcoming spaces for others to explore, connect, and serve community. You were my first teachers and continue to be my daily mentors. My hope is that this work advances your noble efforts and honors what you hold most dear.

Special thanks to the Foundation for Self Leadership for your generous support, enthusiastic partnership, and steadfast encouragement to realize our vision to bring the gifts of IFS to schools around the world. And abundant gratitude to Richard Schwartz, who has inspired expansive possibilities for individual and collective healing and growth through the IFS model.

Table of Contents

Foreword

I'm honored to write this foreword because I'm so grateful to Joanna Curry-Sartori for the movement that she has created.

There was a point in the early years of developing the Internal Family Systems (IFS) model when I realized that it wasn't simply a form of psychotherapy, but instead, had larger implications. What if not just psychotherapy clients, but people in general, accepted that they had parts, and that those parts needed and merited their love and compassion rather than their fear, hatred, or disdain? What if everyone knew that, at their essence, they were the wonderful C words of Self: calm, curiosity, compassion, confidence, courage, clarity, creativity, and connectedness? What if, from a young age, they learned to be Self-led and to relate to one another from that beautiful essence? What if Self-energy permeated schools such that teachers and administrators led from Self could help their students do the same?

It was an intriguing vision, but one that seemed far out of reach. At the time, I was doing family and individual therapy as well as some training and research for an institute in Chicago. I had no training in education and no connections to school systems, and all my students were—like me—therapists. I felt hopeful, however, when Ralph Cohen became enamored with IFS and infused it in his marriage and family therapy master's program at Central Connecticut State University. I hoped one of his students would be inspired to bring it into schools.

And that is just what happened. Joanna came to Ralph's program with years of experience working with young people and a conviction to improve the way schools operated. As you'll see in the preface of this book, this conviction was derived from growing up in a family of educators and from some negative personal experiences in schools.

Joanna also got IFS in a deep way and quickly caught the vision of how it could make that difference. She saw the power of IFS as a healing modality but knew that it had to be simplified if it were to be implemented in education. So she developed the practice that is the centerpiece of this book: PAUSE.

The PAUSE model is an easy-to-learn practice that helps teachers, administrators, and students notice when parts of them are activated so they can then return to Self-leadership. In experimenting with bringing PAUSE to schools, Joanna learned early on that teaching it as an emotional regulation and social skill development tool to students alone would be inadequate, as the goal was to change the whole culture of a school. If teachers cannot stay in Self when students act up, the students will be less inclined to use PAUSE themselves.

Thus, her vision was broader than mine in those early days. I was merely hoping that kids could learn to access Self and to nurture rather than hate their parts when they were hurt or shamed. Because of her extensive work in schools, Joanna knew that for any change to be maintained, all levels of the system need to buy in and to practice.

I've been thrilled to watch from the sidelines as she has taken this dream and run with it. She first infused over 100 schools across Connecticut and the United States with the IFS-based PAUSE program that she details in this book. She then organized the Self Leadership Collaborative, a team with enormous expertise in IFS and education, to spread PAUSE globally, and it is having enormous success.

In this book, Joanna not only describes IFS and her PAUSE adaptation in a clear and understandable way, but she interlaces examples with which everyone connected to schools can identify, including poignant examples from her own life. The book also includes diagrams that help the reader visualize the content, inspiring testimonials from people who have tried it and are thrilled with the results, and exercises so readers can experience it. In other words, Joanna is a talented teacher who knows how to convey the material in a practical and useful fashion that addresses many learning styles.

I am so impressed with this book that I plan to recommend it to anyone who wants a clear model for how IFS can be applied outside of psychotherapy. We have ambitions to expand IFS and Self-leadership beyond the limits of psychotherapy to areas like medicine, social activism, business and political leadership, and more, and this book is a great template for that expansion.

Again, I'm so grateful to Joanna and her team for paving the way, and for the substantial foothold they have already established in the crucial field of education.

—RICHARD SCHWARTZ, ***Founder of Internal Family Systems Therapy***

Preface

I was raised in a family of educators. Together we nurtured the conviction that education provides the tools and possibility to cultivate hope, change, and peace in the world. I attended what was recognized as an excellent public school. Along with the many strengths of the education I received, I found myself grappling with a challenging daily dynamic by middle school. Mean words, exclusive games, and fear of judgment colored my social experience with classmates. I focused on the challenge of performing well academically but often ended up anxious about grades, thus losing sight of the love of learning my family so cherished. I was puzzled. Despite some of my interactions with my classmates, I knew they were, at their core, good people, and my teachers were bright, dedicated, and sincere. With these people involved, why wasn't the system creating a consistently safe and inspiring learning environment? Where did we as a community get stuck?

By eighth grade, I was convinced that the experience of education could be different. In a speech contest, I stood before the judges and painted a picture of a classroom with children who were joyful, creative, and collaborative. They were thriving. I not only longed for this experience of well-being for myself but wished this gift for all children. A seed was planted; I wanted to know how we could realize this vision.

I was fortunate as a teenager to have numerous experiences of thriving in which I found a place of wholeness within myself. I experienced rich, authentic friendships that in one minute would take me into deep contemplation and the next send me into cascades of laughter. I had the privilege to travel to far corners of our world, immersing myself in nature's beauty and delighting in the world's cultures. In all of this, I tasted fulfilling moments of joy, peace, and interconnection. Perhaps most profound was the rare opportunity I had to venture on personal growth retreats, where I realized my power to be my own best friend, to be with my thoughts and feelings while settling into a core place within myself—a place of *being* rather than *doing*, a place where I experienced I was worthy and lovable. When I settled into this inner space, I discovered a foundation of self-confidence and self-compassion. When connected to this resource, I found I was more engaged, creative, and motivated in my work—I could approach my schoolwork and daily life with a sense of enthusiasm and wonder, believing in the value of what I had to contribute. How powerful to know this as an adolescent!

These experiences nurtured a conviction that revealed what was possible for me in my life, but more than that, it demonstrated to me the gifts that reside in every human heart, the inner resources that are our birthright, the state of being we can all contact if we have the road map. This understanding had nothing to do with adopting specific beliefs or philosophy; it was simply my lived experience. With this discovery, I decided to dedicate myself to exploring how I could live from this core inner foundation and support others to experience the same.

After graduating from college with a degree in the humanities, I spent 13 years working at a not-for-profit foundation focused on teaching the integration of practical habits for emotional and relational health in daily life. With roles as a teacher, curriculum developer, and program director, my focus eventually centered on young people—and a few significant questions: How can we meet people early in their lives and help them find pathways to their inner capacity and a life rich with authentic connections? How might this support them to confidently embrace their unique gifts and contribute their full potential to society? These inquiries led me to pursue a master's degree as a marriage and family therapist, and I soon took a role as a school-based community therapist. Since 2010, I've been working with school communities to discover how we can nurture social skills and emotional capacity in school settings. I have been hands-on with individual students, managed student groups during lunches, presented in staff meetings and PTO gatherings, collaborated with administrators, and consulted for whole-school well-being. Throughout this journey, I investigated what could bring forth the inherent potential I knew each individual, family, and school community possessed. If we could find this key, how might this transform the experience of education?

Initially, I focused on teaching techniques to increase self-regulation and effective engagement through stress management. Having studied the relaxation response and practiced self-relaxation since I was a teenager, it came naturally, and I knew personally the profound benefits of the practice. I presented stress management concepts to school staff, and they expressed relief. I implemented lessons in classrooms, so students learned to breathe, calm their emotions, and refocus on school work. Parents and guardians would even report that their children were teaching them new skills to pause and calm down. This was progress in the right direction!

But with time, it was also apparent that the approach was not complete. My efforts were benefiting some people, but it was not consistently translating into the flow of everyday experience. There were disconnects. For example, perhaps a student was sent to the "calm corner" when they were upset and then were invited back in the circle once they'd settled down. But what about understanding the reason for the strong emotions that had come up in the first place? How could adults and students have a safe environment *and* an effective way to discuss their strong emotions and "disruptive" behavior? In other instances, I watched well-meaning teachers read relaxation scripts to their students, but it would come out rushed and abrupt. Students would soon develop a dislike of these exercises, saying things like "It's so annoying! It doesn't work." Why? The teacher was so focused on delivering the techniques to their students that they skipped over themselves entirely. Meanwhile, teachers were stressed, overwhelmed, and disheartened that their familiar toolkit for getting cooperation wasn't working. They wanted new solutions for managing students' emotions, building resilience, and eliciting productive social engagement. On the other side of the school, the principal and social worker were learning other protocols for intervention and trauma-informed care. Many important efforts were underway, but they often lacked cohesion, a shared language, and a consistent process. What was the North Star to develop the essential emotional resilience and relational skills that were necessary for a successful learning experience? What was the fabric that would weave together a healthy, sustainable school culture?

While asking these questions, I was studying the Internal Family Systems (IFS) model for use as a psychotherapist. In IFS, I found a simple, profound, and efficient framework to understand and work with the dynamics of our inner psychology. It offered a paradigm and a model through which to understand and relate to the breadth of human experience. It integrated an understanding of our optimal state of functioning while also explaining the diverse and sometimes concerning patterns of behavior that block our effective, everyday functioning.

While I started to use IFS in my private practice with clients, I also explored its relevance in my own family life, in the relationships I had with my husband and my young son. It offered the fresh approach I needed to notice myself in moments when I was activated, to step back and shift into a more calm and effective way of being. As I experienced personal benefits, I recognized the immense gift that IFS could offer schools—not only for students, but also for school staff and the school system as a whole. Appreciating that IFS could offer an umbrella for holistic well-being in schools, I was joined by fellow IFS colleagues to develop a school framework inspired by IFS practices and principles, an approach that starts with the well-being of *us*—the adults in the system.

There have been many, many people with me on this journey—exceptional colleagues from around the world who have simultaneously piloted the applications of IFS for educators and school communities. We experimented, explored, shared best practices, at times stumbled, and then discovered breakthroughs. This book represents our best practices to date, especially those that help us to nurture our own well-being. After all, how we show up and interact each day with young people models and coaches healthy emotional skills—how we engage with students moment to moment serves as the ultimate lesson, perhaps even more than any formal curriculum. We have endeavored to distill and codify essential concepts and skills that can allow anyone working with schools to follow a consistent IFS-inspired road map to cultivate emotional health and relational capacity as a community. At the same time, the approach is designed to be flexible and responsive to each community, circumstance, and individual. It's also important to note that this is a work in progress. If we are to stay true to this model—to be present and responsive to ourselves, our community, and our world—this approach will be forever evolving. With that said, it is offered to you here, at this time, in this form, with the hope it can bring relief from that which obstructs learning while supporting you and your community to realize your innate potential and collective purpose.

Introduction

Pause and Reflect

- What is the real curiosity or hope that inspired you to open this book?
  - What are you needing right now to care for yourself and feel well-being inside?
  - What are you wishing for the students and colleagues in your community?
  - What do you secretly dare to hope for our schools and our world?

What does it look like in a moment when things are going well at school? Recall a simple everyday instance with others at school, a moment when you were able to show up as your best self. Perhaps you were able to stay calm amid the classroom chaos and patiently coached a discouraged student. Maybe you responded compassionately to an upset parent. You may have spoken with courage to your administrator or contributed an innovative solution when your team was at an impasse. In this moment, you felt centered, you accessed a space of conviction, love was stronger than fear, and you glimpsed, yet again, the magic that is possible in the sphere of education. Leading from this place, you tapped a space of well-being within you and let this spread to those around you. Although brief and frequently unrecognized, these interactions matter profoundly.

As adults caring for children in schools, we've experienced the power of these exchanges. We know how important it is for students to see us navigate the opportunities and challenges in school settings and to coach them to do the same—to negotiate a disagreement on the playground, tolerate frustration with a new lesson, or acknowledge the fear of being left out. When students interact with intentional educators, they have the opportunity to feel seen, build confidence, identify their motivation, and realize capacity to achieve goals. These simple connections, when woven together, create the fabric of a welcoming, healthy, and productive learning environment. They are the foundation for all we do in the field of education. And these micromoments nourish *our* sense of purpose, inspiring us to stay in our profession and even sustain hope amid challenges that seem never-ending or impossible. Simply put, these moments contain the remarkable power to restore collective well-being and ignite collaborative action for common goals.

Though we cherish these quality interactions, they seem to happen rarely, desperately stuck between the far more common moments of overwhelm, discouragement, disconnection, and conflict. How do we nourish the positive interactions as a way to create engagement every day? How do we find and focus on what is in our power?

It is extraordinarily powerful when we show up as our best self in interactions, not because of what we are *doing* but because of how we are *being* together in these moments. This internal exploration begins with attending to our own experience of well-being, to how we recenter amid the stressors in school. As we integrate the practices offered in this book, our everyday interactions with fellow adults and students can become more calm, connected, and effective. We can lead harmonious interactions that unlock learning and create a more productive learning environment. When practiced with others in our community, this book can provide the power to nurture mental health, compassionate connections, and collaborative action as a shared culture, one person and one interaction at a time.

Appreciating the Need

A part of you may be curious and even excited about what you've read so far. *Might it really possible this book offers relief, a way to reenergize my purpose and to contribute to my community?* But other parts of you may believe these quality moments are more a matter of good luck or dependent on external factors. Finally, you might wonder how this approach could be different from all the other models, techniques, and curricula you've tried. It's not surprising that you're hearing from these parts of you. In our different roles as educators, administrators, mental health counselors, and community leaders, many of us are stretched thin, if not severely overwhelmed, frustrated, and exhausted, by the mounting demands of our profession and the condition of the educational system as a whole. Studies reflect what we experience and report daily: Many of us are experiencing increasing levels of depression, anxiety and burnout (Agyapong et al., 2022). In this state, we are not able to show up at our best—calm, creative, and courageous—to nurture our young people, many of whom are also struggling. We don't have the capacity to work optimally together to address the issues that need our attention. Not seeing change in sight, many are leaving the profession in spite of years in the field, extensive training, and deep dedication to students. Where are we stuck and what do we need? Are there possibilities we haven't tried?

A Fresh Paradigm: IFS

The challenges we face in school communities are real, complex, and deep. This book does not claim to be a magic wand, but it does offer a fresh paradigm to understand the dynamics at play within and between us, and it offers a clear road map to guide the significant interactions that fill our days. In a sense, this approach isn't new but integrates best practices from many fields, reflecting what we do intuitively on our best days. At the same time, the approach offered in this book is uniquely inspired by IFS, a groundbreaking psychological framework and a revolutionary paradigm to understand our relationship with ourselves and others.

IFS was developed by Dr. Richard Schwartz. In the 1980s, Schwartz was working as a family therapist and finding that traditional models of therapy were not giving his clients relief. Boldly, Schwartz decided to let go of his agenda and listen deeply as his clients guided him through their inner experience. From this, he extracted a new way to describe the dynamics of our inner lives and developed a powerful process to nurture healthy relationships with ourselves. With the creation of IFS, Schwartz (2021) called for a fundamental change in how humanity is viewed, one that "releases the collaboration and caring that lives in our hearts" (p. 3). Over time, many have recognized that the essential concepts in IFS are not only relevant in the psychotherapeutic space, but also offer a framework to understand human nature and everyday relationships, including those in schools.

Since 2013, I have led a global initiative, collaborating with educators from around the world, to adapt IFS specifically for implementation by adults caring for children in school settings. With a generous grant from the Foundation for Self-Leadership, the nonprofit arm of IFS, my team and I built a framework to apply IFS as a systemic model in schools. A recent qualitative research study (Johnson et al., in press) found that participating in the model enhanced teachers' ability to regulate their emotions, reduce stress, and improve their relationships with students. My approach, which you will learn through this book, offers an intuitive process and simple practices to build social skills competency and emotional resourcefulness through the quality of our everyday relationships.

"IFS has proven to be a universal model, shedding light on the dialogue and conflicts that take place within us when we think, debate with ourselves, and make decisions. This inner experience has cross-cultural relevance and goes beyond national and cultural boundaries. The IFS model has the capacity to transform the way we see ourselves and understand each other. It can thus promote harmony between parents and children, teachers and students, while advancing peace in the whole school environment, within communities, nations, and beyond."

—**Chady Rahme,** associate professor at Notre Dame University–Louaize, Lebanon, and the leader of the Ithraa Center for Training (Lebanon branch)

IFS Core Concepts

As you will discover in this book, I have extracted two core concepts from IFS to apply in school settings. These concepts can transform our perceptions and everyday lived experience and impact how we respond to them.

The Self

The first concept is that we all possess a core *Self*; this is our inner home base, that sense we have when we say, "I feel like myself today!" While many of us are all too familiar with our stress response, we don't often discuss our physiology when we *aren't* stressed—the natural resting experience and state of mental *health* that we are designed to operate from the majority of the time. In this state of being, we are naturally at ease, focused, and cooperative. It's the optimal state of functioning that many of our school programs strive for so students and staff can be resilient, resourceful, regulated, competent, restorative, productive, and collaborative.

Importantly, we can learn to recognize and access this state on purpose, discovering our natural pathways to shift back to our Self again and again. Building our capacity to lead from Self, what I call *Self-leadership*, opens the door for us all—regardless of age or role—to realize a new way of *being* together. Self-leadership reflects the goal of many programs that develop character, social skills, and emotional regulation in educational settings. It represents the core state of being students and adults need to access to do what is expected in schools, including studying, teaching, listening, sharing, producing, and performing.

There is so much we want our students and teachers to *do* . . .
Our success and capacity to do depends first on how we are *being*.

"I think that Self-leadership is unique in its combination of support for both adults and students. While other programs to build student competency focus on what to *do*, the Self-leadership approach says that we first need to learn how to *be*. It is a model that supports growth through collaboration and peer support. Because of this, Self-leadership offered our school a holistic model and became the 'North Star' we were looking for. And remarkably, this shift in being begins on the inside . . . inside us!"

—**Kirsten Sanderson,** retired elementary teacher and curriculum specialist, Connecticut

At this point, perhaps you like the idea of Self-leadership. At the same time, practical parts of you rise up, reminding you of moments when, in spite of your best efforts, your buttons were pushed or students overreacted. If this state of being Self-led is real and accessible, why do we feel hijacked, reactive, and overtaken by a totally different frame of mind or pattern of behavior? Why doesn't it feel like a simple choice just to shift gears and get back on track to being our centered Self? This brings us to the second concept adapted from IFS: the idea that we all have multiple parts.

Parts

To understand parts, let's unpack what happens when we are stressed. In the face of external stressors—a disruptive student, a judgmental colleague, an ungrateful parent, a demanding administrator—we *perceive* a threat. That is, in some way, we don't feel safe, we don't feel seen and understood, or we feel misjudged, excluded, or criticized. This can knock us off our game and out of a Self-led state. Why does this happen? In these instances, our inner system instinctively moves to protect us. We unconsciously call on the best strategy we know to address a feeling of vulnerability and to get our needs met. These strategies manifest as different parts of us. We've all experienced these different parts that take over to protect us in challenging situations: people pleasing, yelling to get control, shutting down instead of speaking up, organizing perfectly, walling off so we don't get hurt again. Additionally, from a young age, we learn that certain parts of us are considered good and others bad. We are taught to manage or subvert "bad" parts, rarely considering that *all* parts of us developed with a positive intent: to protect us. If we try on this radical and compassionate view, our different parts can be seen as an inner team, each with a role to help us (even if we don't always like the results). We can learn to be our own inner team leader and welcome, understand, and lead all our parts. When we apply the awareness of these parts in our relationship with others, we see that the parts are not the whole person, and that behind these well-intentioned protective parts lies our core Self. In making this shift in perception, we are able to effectively relate to the various parts rising up within us, and others, to return to Self-leadership as our modus operandi.

Let's consider what this looks like in action. Early in my time as a school therapist and consultant, I was called into a classroom by a middle school teacher, who I'll call Christina, to help with some students she found challenging. When I arrived, she was alone on her lunch break, and she recounted what happened that morning when she had introduced a new math concept to her students. Only five minutes into the lesson, she noticed Maria staring out the window and Carlos and Jazz whispering in the back row. She tried to offer a number of kind reminders, but the students' behaviors recurred. She then shifted into "lay-down-the-law" mode and threatened to send them to the principal if they didn't stop. This inspired another student, Annie, to respond, "You guys, this is so totally simple. Just shut up and actually try." With this, Christina yelled for silence, passed out worksheets, and insisted that the students work on their own with no talking for one hour. This caused Maria to shut down, put her head on the desk, and refuse to respond. Carlos and Jazz were separated and just doodled on their papers with pouts on their faces. Annie passed in her worksheet early.

After listening and nodding, I replied, "Wow, that was a tough morning. I can tell how hard you tried, and I imagine it was so frustrating."

Christina made eye contact with me and softened as she felt more connected. "When the students started reacting, it really pushed my buttons. At first, a part of me tried so hard to be patient and nice to soften them. When they didn't respond, I felt out of control, and it actually hurt. I stayed up late last night preparing for this lesson. So then I just reverted to control mode. And of course that didn't work!" She laughed.

I responded, "All these different parts of you make a lot of sense. I get it. You're truly trying your best and care so much! What do you need?"

"I suppose simply the acknowledgment you just gave me. That really helped. I am so hard on myself. It never feels like what I do is good enough. And, I need to remember these are kids. They are different on different days, also trying their best to get their needs met. Not one of them is bad!"

From a place of more compassion, confidence, and clarity, Christina went on to describe the different personalities of this group of students, sharing her questions and concerns about them. Listening, I started to reflect back to her the students' behavior in terms of the different parts of them she described.

I wondered aloud, "It seems like a part of Maria was distracted. Maybe this was somehow helping her from being in the discomfort of learning something new." I added, "I hear that Carlos was especially chatty. It makes me curious if a part of him is looking to create a bit more fun and connection with his friends, even if another part of him knows that's disruptive."

These reflections further settled Christina. She then started to offer some interesting observations. She shared that the previous day, Carlos was quiet and focused all afternoon. She remarked that just a day later, she was seeing a really different side of him. She added that Maria was one of the sweetest, most cooperative students in her class.

Then with a look of sudden realization, Christina said, "But come to think of it, this 'distraction part' is the part of her that comes up whenever I introduce a new lesson in math." With this, Christina exhaled deeply. She was seeing the different parts of her students that come up in different circumstances and remembering their core goodness.

After lunch, Christina returned to her students to reset. Without judgment, she acknowledged some of the different parts of students that she'd noticed often come up with new math lessons: looking out the window, talking with friends, being playful, trying hard to be good. She expressed understanding that all these parts made sense for middle school students, especially in the face of new material.

She went on to speak for her parts, "I know a part of me got triggered and yelled. I overreacted. I am so sorry. This isn't who I want to be with you. And I want you to know that under this reaction is another part of me that just cares so much about you all and really wants to teach in a way that works for you. I know you don't always want to come to school, but I wonder how we can make it tolerable if not a bit more fun."

She then asked for their suggestions: how they wanted to be together for the next math lesson, and what they could do together to make it more interesting and accessible. This vulnerability hooked the students, and as they leaned in, the feeling in the room shifted. They were a community.

What happened in this story of Christina? What worked? In conversation with me, Christina first paused. She needed to step back, take a breath, and get perspective before she was ready to respond. In this space, she noticed her own inner reaction as an adult. She recognized different, understandable parts coming up within her. With my acknowledgment, she let these parts settle back a bit, as if clearing space inside. This radically shifted her view of the students she was working with; she could then see them in their wholeness and complexity, their goodness and their understandable needs. In turn, she activated a sense of compassion and a fresh capacity to consider what everyone needed next, further facilitating a subtle but profound change in how Christina was *being* as she returned to *doing*—in this case, the action of teaching and leading her students. As you read this account, perhaps a part of you is nodding in recognition. *Yes, this is what I do instinctively on my best days.* Exactly! This organic process is captured in PAUSE for Self-Leadership™, a model to support us individually and collectively to discover our power to operate consciously together.

PAUSE for Self-Leadership

The PAUSE for Self-Leadership™ model is designed to cultivate Self-leadership as our way of operating in the ever-changing, button-pushing, often chaotic juggling act that is life at school. I developed the acronym PAUSE as an at-your-fingertips companion to access Self-leadership and to guide you through the complex play of activated parts even in the simplest school-based interactions. Each element of PAUSE strengthens your connection to Self-leadership in yourself, in your relationship to others, and as you navigate everyday actions. Following the PAUSE model brings a realization of your power to care for your own well-being and to call forth the true potential in those around you simply by *how* you engage in moment-to-moment interactions. In this way, PAUSE is not more to do, but a road map to shift how we are *being* amid all we already do.

These are the five steps of PAUSE and how we will study them in this book:

- ***Pause*** **and notice your state of being and connection to your Self:** What is happening outside and inside you? Step back, breathe, get perspective, and connect to Self. You will learn to recognize your unique signs when you are in a regulated physiological state versus when you are in an activated, stressed state. Then you will explore your personal pathways to pause and return to your core Self, even amid a busy day.
- **Be** ***Aware*** **of your inner response and underlying needs (your parts):** Where are *you* coming from? You will consider your parts (response patterns), including how you recognize them, how they show up at school, and how they drive your responses. Then you will learn simple processes to build a healthy relationship with yourself on the inside and to lead your inner team of parts.
- ***Understand*** **each other:** Where are *others* coming from? You will develop the powerful ability to see parts at play in your relationships with others, recognizing patterns of interaction that escalate tension and those that block productive communication. Then you will try out simple, practical skills to listen so that others feel heard and to speak so others understand your perspective and needs.
- ***Search*** **for solutions that will serve the situation:** What might be possible? The P, A, and U help you to access greater Self-leadership with others so that you are positioned to look at the situation together, seeing what is needed and what will serve the greater good. Delving into the S, you will learn how to most effectively search: brainstorming options, considering what is in your power, and collaborating to choose effective action.
- ***Experiment*** **with Self-led action:** What can you try? You will discover how to take the fruits of the PAUSE process into action, engaging mindfully and then reflecting on the fruits of your action for continuous learning.

Once comfortable with each element of the PAUSE model, you will develop fluency to follow the steps as a process to guide you and others to realize Self-led interactions. Picture that even in the face of the most challenging or perplexing situations—a resistant student, interpersonal conflict, major curricular changes—you now have a practical process to follow so you can show up as your calm Self, establish connection with others, and effectively lead collaborative action in your community. This is the gift of PAUSE.

This book offers a blueprint to practice living with greater Self-leadership in school settings—to understand what is happening organically on our best days, what parts are hijacking us on our worst, and how to hold self-compassion throughout. As we apply Self-leadership in one interaction, one situation at a time, we cultivate a new way of functioning together that nurtures the heart of school culture and climate. It's not a top-down agenda from an administrator or something we "should" do for self-care, but an invitation to explore and improve our relationship with ourselves and each other. We can practice the elements of the PAUSE model so with time, we are skillful to recenter in Self-leadership in the flow of everyday life experience. The model builds a new way of *being* that reflects social and emotional health, eventually creating the foundation for a new way of *doing*. With this, we find the possibility for a different experience for ourselves, restoring a sense of purpose, joy, and enthusiasm at the heart of our work and releasing our full capacity to be of service to our students and our communities. Let's begin the journey!

Stories from the Field

The Answer Is in Me

Erica Hermann, LCSW, LAC, is a social worker at an alternative high school in Colorado.

As a school social worker, mother, wife, and individual, I have a passion for learning about and practicing approaches to help my students, colleagues, family, and myself achieve optimal mental health and well-being. After years of applying different best-practice modalities in my various roles, while I would often see a short-term positive impact, I also began to feel a bit disillusioned. The ongoing effort and recall that it took to apply the right modality at the right time didn't feel sustainable for myself, my students, my school community, or my family. IFS and the PAUSE approach have been a complete game changer for me. What's different about this approach is that the "answer" isn't somewhere out there—some new concept or curriculum that we all have to work hard to learn, remember, and practice. Ultimately, the answer lies inside each one of us, in the core Self that every single human on earth has.

It was such a relief to realize that not only do I have everything I need inside of me to guide my personal life, but I also don't need to be the expert on the lives of my family members, students, and colleagues, constantly rifling through the various social-emotional modalities to see what will work best for them. Instead, they too possess this core Self, and if I can help them learn to access and lead from this wise, loving place within, the healing and growth will happen naturally. The PAUSE approach complements all of the wonderful life skills programs already happening in schools, and it makes certain core concepts, such as empathy, self-compassion, mindfulness, and healthy conflict resolution, more tangible and easier to practice.

After more than a decade of working in schools and enthusiastically practicing many of the cutting-edge social-emotional modalities, I truly believe that the PAUSE approach holds within it everything that we need to equip our students, staff, and school cultures with true social-emotional health, growth, and vitality. Working in education is exciting because of the great impact we can have on our future generation; to imagine a world in which our children carry forth Self-leadership into their lives, thus impacting everyone around them, is nothing short of thrilling, and it fills me with enormous hope.

Invitations to Practice

At the end of each chapter, you will find an assortment of practices like these to help you pause, explore, and directly apply the material you have learned in the previous pages. I encourage you to choose at least one practice that inspires you. Appreciating that we have different learning styles, you will find an invitation to write, visualize, embody, enact, or practice your learning in other ways.

WRITE: *Note Your Responses So Far*

As you consider the possibilities of learning about Self-leadership and the PAUSE model, what responses come up for you? Are there hopes, doubts, excitement, concerns? List your reflections, uncensored, just acknowledging the different parts of you.

EMBODY: *Reflect on Your Why*

Take a walk and ask yourself what you long for. What do you wish for yourself, your students, and your school community? What is your vision for what might be possible? What is your why for reading this book, and more importantly, for doing this work?

CONTEMPLATE: *The PAUSE Model*

Take a look at the PAUSE model that is simplified in the following image. Review the steps and notice what makes sense to you. How might this be similar to what you already do intuitively on your best days? Picture yourself following these steps in an upcoming interaction. What might be the effect?

The PAUSE for Self-Leadership Model™

Pause: What is happening outside and inside?
Step back, breathe, and connect to Self.

Aware of myself: Where am I coming from?
Notice my parts: thoughts, feelings, perspectives, and needs.

Understand each other: Where are others coming from?
Listen from Self and speak for parts.

Search for solutions: What might be possible?
Brainstorm what is for the good of all and identify what is in our power.

Experiment: What can we try?
Act purposefully, acknowledge accomplishments, and be curious to learn.

ACT: *Acknowledge Strengths to Build On*

As you move through your day, notice what is already working. What are you *already* doing and what is *already* happening that supports well-being and healthy interactions for you, your students, and your school community? Acknowledge what's working, as we often overlook this, preoccupied with what is still not good enough. Once you see what is working, you know the strengths you can build upon.

CHAPTER 1

Pause: Connecting to Self-Leadership

Pause and Reflect

- Return to a moment when you experienced being your best or truest self at school. As this experience comes to mind, shift your focus from what you were externally *doing* to how you were internally *being* in that moment:
  - Recall your inner state of thoughts, feelings, or physical sensations.
  - What words best describe your inner state?

You've been working after school with a student. You are intentionally staying *calm and patient* as they struggle with a new concept. Then comes that magical moment when you see the light of comprehension dawn in their eyes. You are listening to a colleague who you sometimes find activating and challenging. You listen with *compassion*, without the need to fix, and you watch as they let their guard down for a moment; there is a palpable sense of *connection*. At a parent-teacher conference, you *confidently* share your approach to support a student and express *curiosity* to better understand their needs. A space of *collaboration* opens, and a parent shares a vulnerable personal story that puts their child's challenging behavior into perspective.

These are moments that remind us of who we are, what we are capable of, and how we can impact a situation for ourselves and others; these moments renew a sense of purpose and motivate us to continue on in spite of the many challenges we face each day.

Our students also have these moments when they experience being their best selves. Even the seemingly "difficult" students have days when they kindly share their pencil with a classmate, calmly persist to learn a new skill even when they feel confused, or graciously express thanks after we help them. When students experience this capacity in themselves, when they touch their innate goodness, they feel competent, valuable, and hopeful. This fuels learning. What if we, adults and young people alike, could experience these moments more often, and with practice, deliberately shift into this way of being? Our ability to practice accessing and living from this optimal state of Self-leadership is at the heart of practicing the PAUSE model. As we develop our understanding and capacity to lead from Self, we will be better positioned to support students in doing the same.

In this chapter, we will:

- Explore the experience of Self and benefits of Self-leadership
- Understand the internal and external challenges that can obstruct our connection to Self-leadership
- Consider personal practices that can help us access a more Self-led state

Self: A Familiar Experience

Regardless of our age, we can all relate to moments when we felt like "ourselves." We refer to this in our everyday language in a variety of ways; we speak of being "on our game," "in the zone," or simply, "That's when I'm my real self." Thus, *Self* is how we will refer to this optimal state of being. We've capitalized the word to differentiate it from the passing moods that can overtake the many versions of ourselves. While saying, "I'm anxious" or "That's an angry person" identifies aspects of an individual's personality, these phrases do not represent the totality of who we are. In contrast, Self is an underlying experience of who we are that remains constant, even as different moods arise and subside. Self is also an inner resource that's ever-present, just as the sun is always there even if covered by clouds. Though we each have a unique way to describe when we are "there," we are all familiar with it because it is a physiological state of being inherent in all of us—a birthright—wired into the very makeup of our bodies.

What is this physiological experience of being in Self? Our bodies are wise, and when we perceive we are in a safe situation with our basic needs cared for and a sense of belonging, our body is at ease. When we investigate what is happening in our bodies in these moments, we can measure a slower heart rate, deeper breathing, relaxed muscles, a stronger immune system, and an increase in hormones associated with happiness (Alexander et al., 2021). When we perceive safety, our body supports calm behavioral states, social engagement, growth, and restoration (Porges, 2007). This physiological state also has a significant impact on our brains. In this relaxed state, the brain can function optimally. The prefrontal cortex, the portion of the brain especially unique in humans, is "online," supporting us to engage in more subtle and complex human endeavors, such as learning, remembering, problem-solving, conflict resolution, and compassionate communication. These are the very capacities essential for us to succeed in school, whether as adults or students.

Consider the benefits of operating from this optimal physiology as an educator or student. When we remain in Self while confronting stressors and challenges at school, we can maintain awareness of our abilities and resources and contribute our full potential. We recognize that while we are facing an external change or unknown challenge, we can handle it. Assured, we proceed to engage productively, and despite the difficulty, emerge with increased confidence and resilience. As a result, we develop a positive story of ourselves as someone capable and inherently worthy.

The more we live our days in this integrated physiology, the more we arrive at the end of our days feeling refreshed and fulfilled. And the benefit doesn't stop with us. As social creatures traveling through life together, we constantly send each other cues not only through words but through our nervous systems. When one of us is in a calm, regulated space, we can spread this experience to all those we touch. We can be the source of a contagion, sharing our state of well-being.

Just holding the simple conviction that we all possess the state of Self can be a game changer in the educational environment. Let's picture what impact it might have in our schools if adults and students alike practiced accessing their core Self and even called it forth in each other. Consider these examples of individuals being Self-led. Note that doing so is not some dramatic shift, but something we are already familiar with:

- A student receives a math test, and for a moment, they feel scared, even slightly paralyzed. Then they remember they can pause, take a breath to *calm* themselves, and say to themselves, "It's okay. One step at a time. Just do my best." With a bit more *confidence,* they start the test.

- A group of students at recess organize a game of tag. Juan notices that Elijah, a student with special needs, is sitting alone watching them. Juan finds a place of *courage* inside. He is aware it might not be a popular suggestion, but he says, "Hey guys, let's make it so Elijah can join too." Moved by his *compassion*, the other kids follow Juan's lead.
- A teacher, exasperated by multiple dysregulated students, catches the moment that she almost loses it and tells the students she needs to take a break for a moment. *Creativity* arises and she invites the students to join her. They sit at their desks and count three breaths while they feel their bellies go up and down. The teacher regains *clarity* on what needs attention and simultaneously supports greater focus and readiness with the students.
- An administrator has a student in his office who has exhibited disruptive behavior during a testing situation. Rather than jump to conclusions and punish the student, he asks a question to understand. *Compassion* rises up as he hears the student's side of the story, realizing how deeply this child wants acknowledgment. Feeling *connected,* the two *creatively* brainstorm a new way for the student to get his needs met.
- An impatient parent shows up in the front office of the school, frustrated their child isn't waiting and ready for pickup. The receptionist stays *calm*, takes action to call the student from class, and reassures the parent. Next, they find *curiosity* to ask the parent how they are doing. This allows the parent to acknowledge they're actually overwhelmed for other reasons entirely: their brother is in the hospital for surgery.

As we reflect on these examples and our own experience of being our best Self, we can recognize our unique experience and find our own language to describe this state of being. At the same time, many of us choose common words to describe being in Self. Take a moment to notice the italicized words in the examples above. These words (*calm, compassionate, courageous, curious, confident, clear, creative, connected*) are known in IFS theory as the 8 C qualities of Self (the

8 Cs). These common descriptors of the experience of being in Self supply us with a shared language as we study and experience Self. Interestingly, the 8 Cs are often already highlighted in our school communities; these words and their synonyms are commonly expressed as school values or community norms. Let's explore these 8 C qualities a bit more deeply, and as we do, consider how they relate to your experience, personally and in your learning community. The following graphic shows the 8 Cs of Self depicted as the sun. Just like the rays of the sun radiating within the solar system, we experience and share the C qualities when we are connected with our core true Self.

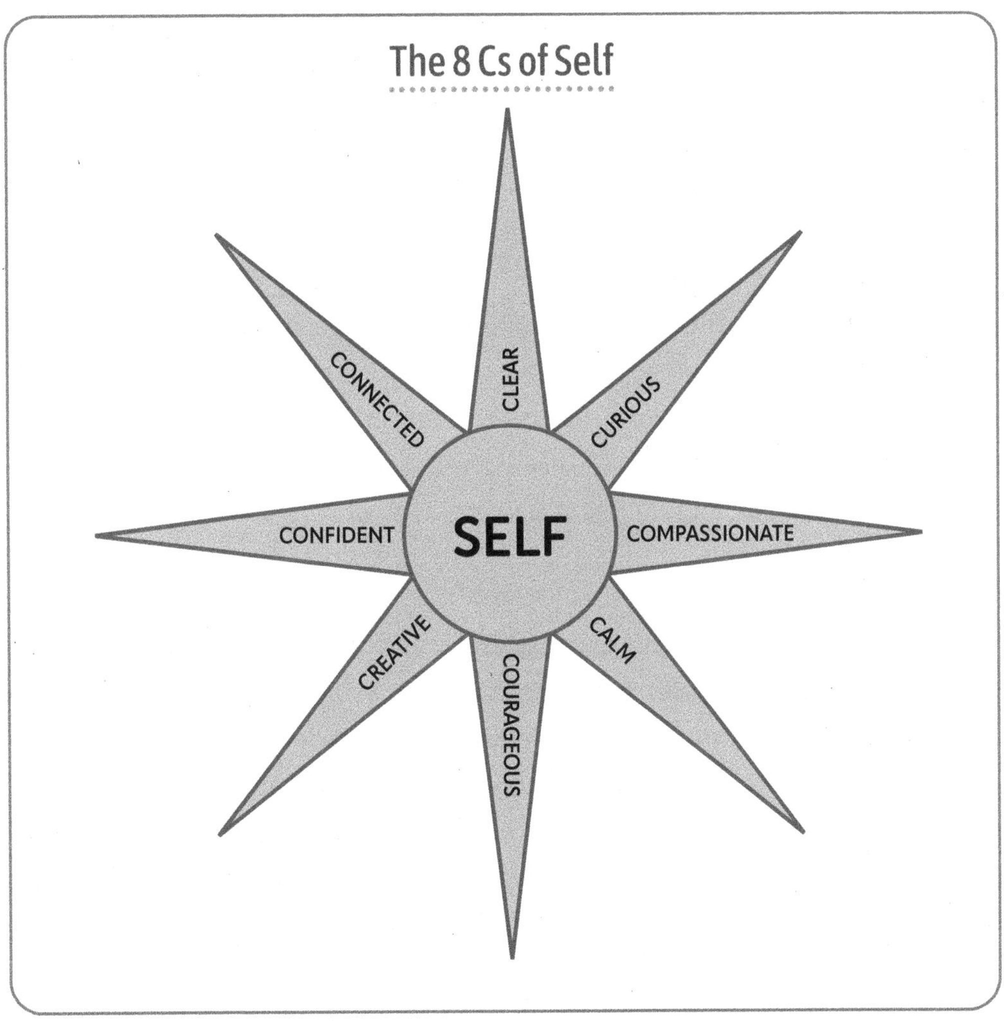

Pause and Reflect

- The next portion of this chapter dives deeper into each of the 8 qualities of Self:
  - As you review their definitions, consider when you have personally experienced these qualities.
  - Think about how you have seen them show up in others.
  - Imagine what might be possible if these qualities were recognized and cultivated intentionally by you and others in your school community.

The 8 Qualities of Self

CLARITY

Clarity arises when we see a situation more objectively, without assumptions and preconceptions that confuse or distort. Clarity may be experienced as an inner state of mind, a sense of ease, or tranquility in which we know what's needed and have conviction to act.

For example, when tensions rise in a team meeting regarding how to roll out a new initiative, you step back to breathe and calm your system, appreciate the different perspectives, and suggest a next step that works for all.

COURAGE

When we are courageous, we step out of self-protective instincts and embrace the calling of the moment to act with integrity, care, and purpose. When we are in courage, we can be aware of our fear—our worries, anxieties, and what-ifs—and then consciously choose to let something deeper, stronger, and truer take the lead.

For example, you want to speak with your supervisor to ask for certain essential resources but fear they will judge you as incompetent or difficult. By recognizing your worth and the rationale for your request, you are able to respectfully assert your needs.

CONFIDENCE

Confidence gives us the power to remember who we are and act from this conviction. We see our own innate goodness, acknowledge our own effort, value our unique traits and gifts, recognize our positive intention, and own our capacities. Connected to our personal dignity, we face life's challenges with poise and embrace the lessons that can nourish us moving forward.

For example, you are invited to lead a brief self-reflection at the start of your next staff meeting. You worry about how you might be judged but proceed by finding conviction from your own experience and your wish to support well-being in your community.

CALM

In calm, we experience a place inside us that possesses peace, steadiness, and quietude. We notice a palpable shift in our body: tension relaxes, waves of emotion subside, and our mind clears. When the inevitable activators of life present, calm gives us the power to step back rather than react in automatic or extreme ways.

For example, a student is sick in the classroom and while you try to contact the nurse, another group of students starts goofing around with scissors. Feeling a rush of overwhelm, you briefly pause, prioritize what needs your attention, and attend to the safety of your students without agitating the situation further.

CURIOSITY

Curiosity allows us to approach life from a state of wonder, wishing to learn and wanting to understand. Free of judgment, assumptions, or labels, curiosity supports us in being open-minded, seeing multiple perspectives, and exploring the heart of a situation. Curiosity allows space for connection and trust to grow between us and others.

For example, you are mediating a conversation between two students who just had an argument during lunch. You recognize your inclination to take sides and instead listen with an interest in where each student is coming from.

COMPASSION

The heart of compassion is our power to *be with* another, to hold and honor their experience without needing to assess, rescue, or fix. We remain anchored to our own center and offer love that supports another in finding their own power to heal.

For example, a colleague confesses to you that they received a critical review from administration that they feel is unfair. While you don't know the details of their performance and can't change the situation, you sit with them, listen, and understand their perspective so they feel less alone.

CREATIVITY

In creativity, we tap into our imagination and listen to the inspiration flowing through us in the form of generative possibilities or alternative solutions. Creativity allows us to discover optimal ways to express ourselves and collaborate in community.

For example, a key team member is suddenly out on family medical leave. As a team, you come together to consider how you can adapt and cover their responsibilities.

CONNECTEDNESS

Connectedness evokes the image of two or more entities being linked, influencing each other and engaging in mutual nourishment. Connection reminds us of the great and complex web of life that we impact and that continually influences us in return.

For example, there is a sudden and tragic death in the community. Rather than press on as if everything is normal, you gather in community, acknowledge the loss, and take turns expressing your experience.

Self on a Continuum

To reflect on the 8 Cs can be deeply inspiring and energizing. It can also be a bit daunting. Are we supposed to be able to embody *all* these qualities? Keep in mind, we are not expected to access all 8 Cs at once. In fact, sometimes all we need is to connect with just a shred of a single quality—a glimpse of curiosity, a drop of compassion—to significantly shift our experience. What we need is critical mass of Self: enough connection of Self to shift our perception and engage productively with the dynamics of the moment. We can picture that we function on a subtle spectrum that ranges from slightly more Self-led to slightly more stressed, protective, and reactive. We can build our awareness of when and how we tip more toward Self-leadership and notice when we have just a bit more Self on board. We can imagine we have a "Self detector" and use it to uncover signs of Self in ourselves and others. For example, we might notice:

- Physical cues of feeling more at ease, open, or relaxed: Our breath deepens, our shoulders relax, we smile.
- Thoughts and feelings that support a sense of well-being, capacity, and connection: *I can handle this. I am not alone. I am grateful to be here.*
- The results of actions that signal a beneficial impact for all involved: People present as happy to work together, problems feel resolved, and projects advance with greater ease.

Students and adults alike can increase their awareness of the signs of Self, acknowledge these moments, and grow their capacity to access and lead from this state. At a practical level, this sets us up for increased productivity and performance in school activities. At a deeper level, however, we will be able to show up more fully, engage with a higher degree of enthusiasm, confidently work with others, and realize purposeful goals.

Stories from the Field

Bringing Forth Self in Schools

Kena Acuña, MPHE, ACC, is a consultant, leadership coach, and training facilitator in New York.

For over seven years I've been involved in training educators in social-emotional learning and restorative practices in New York City schools. When I learned about IFS, it gave me a language to recognize and articulate what was happening when my work flowed; I was in Self. I've found that when I am able to access the qualities of Self and teach from that place, the training goes smoother and there is greater connection among the circle of participants. Holding love, compassion, and especially curiosity creates spaciousness that invites others to access their own Self. It is in this space that transformation can happen more quickly; protective parts in people realize they can relax when Self is leading. In this, compassion is easily experienced and insights abound.

I've also come to recognize the simple ways that schools intuitively integrate practices that support greater access to Self for the community. For example, it was the first day of a training series on social-emotional learning for educators. I suddenly heard a familiar song come over the classroom loudspeaker. I was puzzled and pleased. The school staff who were sitting in the circle smiled and explained that this song was being used as the "bell" to signify a change of class. It occurred to me how easily we can help students, teachers, and everyone at the school connect to their playful and joyful core through music. The school was helping everyone, including me in that moment, to access Self.

Stress: Disconnection from Self

As we appreciate that the state of Self is innate within us, we may begin to wonder why we don't live in this state all the time. What are the "clouds" that block the sun? To understand this, let's unpack what happens in moments of stress. We are often surrounded by conversations about stress and its effects. We may use the word *stress* to refer to everything from a minor annoyance to major life changes and losses. We may equate external circumstances with our internal experience, as if being stressed out is an inevitable response to life's outer challenges.

Students say, "I have an hour of homework today; [therefore] I am in a really bad mood!"

Teachers chatting in the teachers' lounge say, "The principal is coming to my classroom on Friday to assess me; [therefore] I am a wreck!"

Parents conversing after school might share, "It looks like we are going to have a snow day tomorrow; [therefore] it's too much!"

If we look more closely at these types of responses, we see an external event (e.g., homework, principal's assessment, snow day) and each person's perception of and response to this external event. As we differentiate *external* stressors from our *internal* response, we increase the possibility that we can and will be able to choose our response.

External Stressors

External stressors are inevitable. As soon as one resolves, others arise. Some are more serious while others are more mundane. We try to manage them by preparing, avoiding, or organizing. This may bring a degree of relief, yet we find that there's always something!

Review this list of common external stressors experienced by adults and children. Look for what you relate to and what you would add:

- **School:** projects, assessments, initiatives, homework, relationships
- **Relationships:** misunderstandings, everyday conflict, power differentials
- **Employment and finances:** hiring, firing, job changes, new boss, financial hardships
- **Physical health:** features, weight, illness, death
- **Society:** politics, commercialism, racism, sexism, genderism, division, war
- **Environment:** weather, temperature, natural disasters, climate change
- **Transitions:** birth, death, new house, new job, marriage, divorce

Given the reality that there are external factors we can't control or eliminate no matter how hard we try, what *is* in our power? What can we influence? We often don't realize how much our *inner* perception about the situation impacts our experience and response to what is happening externally.

Our Internal Response to Stress

Our perception of external stressors determines our internal narrative about what is happening, and thus our subsequent response. Let's consider two scenarios for what happens within us when faced with a stressor.

First, if we think, *Something is happening outside of me, and I can handle it and am okay,* what happens? Physically, we remain in what Herbert Benson (1975) identified as the *relaxation response.* Our nervous system is regulated. We continue to function from our whole brain, remaining capable of higher-order thinking and making meaning of our experience in a healthy way. We are able to imagine multiple solutions. We are effective in our response, choosing necessary action proportional to the situation. This is what it looks like to move through a challenging situation in a state of what we are calling *Self-leadership.*

Alternatively, we sometimes see external realities as a threat and think, *I'll never be able to handle this! I just can't cope.* With this perception, our nervous system instinctively moves into either fight, flight, freeze, or fawn mode. We feel unsafe and out of control, so we move to protect ourselves. As this happens, changes occur in our body, such as increased heart rate and rapid breathing. Our brain functioning changes, too. Believing we need to focus on survival, our brain shuts down higher-order thinking and integrated functioning in preference to the efficient survival mode of the lower brain. Originally evolved to help us navigate crises in the wild, this physiological response makes sense: We could run from fire, fight a dangerous opponent, freeze when cornered by a predator, or fawn to appease a perceived threat. Our system is designed to protect us from life-threatening dangers in these ways.

However, in the face of modern-day stressors, such as a teacher being assessed by the principal or a student taking an exam, this physiological response is not proportional or useful. In fact, it often works against us, making us much less effective in responding to the stressor. The essential social and emotional capacities needed for teaching and learning are often subdued if not negated by an active stress response in the body.

The following image demonstrates the two tracks we can take in response to stressors, depending on our perspective. If we pause and take perspective, seen in the upper half of the image, we can steer toward greater Self-leadership. If we perceive a threat and a stress response is activated, as seen in the lower half of the image, we are more likely to veer toward a more self-protective response.

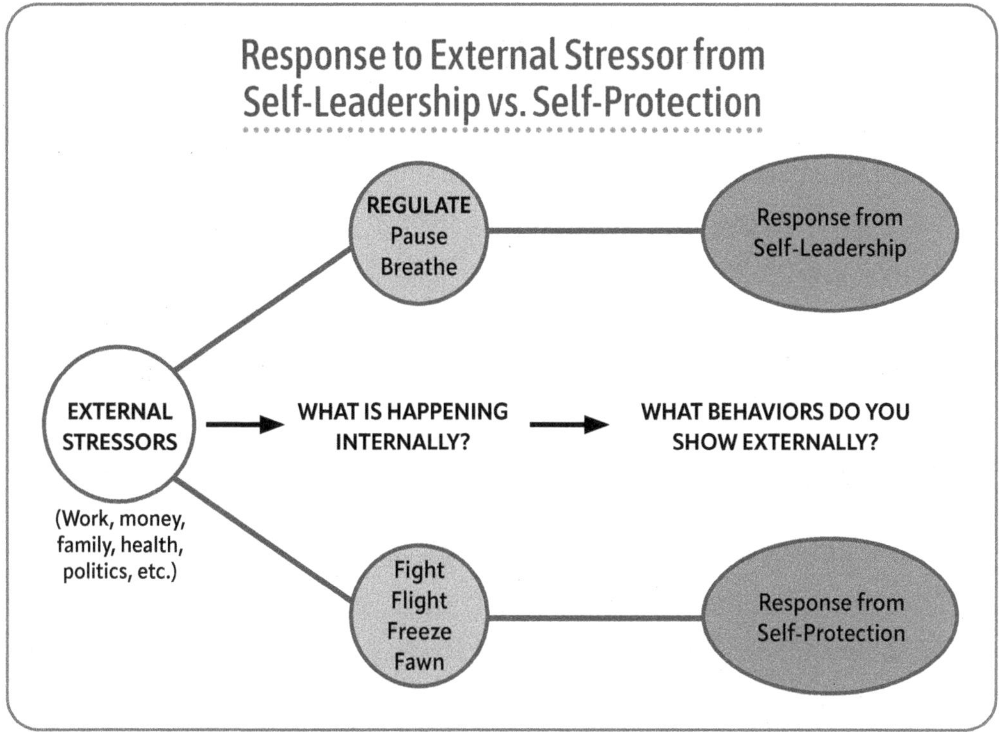

This simple visual gives us some sense of how we may perceive and respond to a threat when confronted with a stressor. In reality, our response is not one of two extreme states—either entirely Self-led or self-protective. Rather, our responses are experienced and manifest on a spectrum; there are times we feel relatively more Self-led and other times we are more self-protective.

The Stress Response in Schools

Our built-in protective response to avoid a sense of vulnerability makes sense; you could even say it's useful. But when this protective mechanism shows up as automatic reactive patterns in adults and students in our schools, it's generally counterproductive. Reflect on these examples and consider how each person felt vulnerable as they perceived a threat and moved to protect themselves:

- A student in the back of the room is talking to his neighbor while his teacher presents new content. Inside, the student is scared he won't understand the new material, so he distracts himself to avoid feeling stupid.
- The school social worker is called to break up an argument erupting on the playground between kids. Afraid the situation could spiral out of control,

she immediately removes recess privileges from both kids for the rest of the week rather than stopping to listen to their side of the story.

- A parent blames their child's teacher for upsetting their child and causing a panic attack. Underneath their accusation, though, the parent feels embarrassed that their child exhibits anxiety.

In moments like these, we feel vulnerable and try to protect ourselves. Ironically, after the fact, we often regret our self-protective actions, and furthermore, we may even be upset with the final result of the situation.

Recognizing the negative impact of a stress response, we may wonder whether these responses are ever appropriate in our modern lives. Certainly, there are times in and out of school when we face realities that are literally and physically dangerous. In these cases, it's understandable and natural that the fight, flight, freeze, or fawn reactions take over: Our instinctual response is helping us defend against or escape actual threats. While this makes sense, many of these moments also benefit if we have greater access to the 8 C qualities of Self. And with that said, the majority of stressors we face in school are not physically threatening, so Self-leadership best serves as our response. In schools, adults and students may be required to take actions like navigating sensitive interactions with others, quickly processing information, deescalating conflict, establishing common ground, or effectively setting boundaries. For these nuanced and sophisticated interactions, we benefit from accessing the 8 C qualities, and with a greater connection to Self-leadership, we can more readily identify the most beneficial response. We can act purposefully and inspire reconnection and repair when there has been rupture. We can identify and take action based on what is in our power. While each person and situation is unique, the access to our Self can transform our response even in school's most intense moments.

Signs of Self and Stress

Just as we study the signals of Self, it's useful to develop our familiarity with the signs that our system is in a stress response. This awareness empowers us to choose our perception and corresponding response.

Pause and Reflect

- Review the following table, which captures a few signs of Self and stress:
  - Identify the signs you relate to. Are there any you would add?
  - Recognize how these signs present in the students you work with. Are there any you would add?

Signs of Self vs. Stress

Inner Leader	Signs of Self and Self-Leadership	Signs of Stress and Self-Protection
Physical	Relaxed muscles, slow heart rate, easy breath, aligned and open body	Clenched muscles, rigid posture, shallow breath, rapid heartbeat, ready to fight, flight, freeze, or fawn
Neuroscience	Whole brain: prefrontal cortex available for learning, memory, conflict resolution, empathy, and higher-order thinking	Survival brain: brain in stress response, parts such as the prefrontal cortex are compromised, often called an *amygdala hijack*
Being/ Attributes	8 Cs: calm, compassionate, courageous, curious, confident, clear, creative, connected	Nervous, judging, afraid, insecure, confused, distracted, defensive, dull, passive
Perception/ Belief	"I am safe, valued, connected, good enough; I am okay."	"I am unsafe, not valued, not connected, not good enough; I am threatened."
Mindset and Motive	Growth-oriented, resilient, solution-based mindset, collaborative, welcoming, oriented toward the good of all, us-focused	Fixed, rigid, all-or-nothing thinking, problem-based mindset, competitive, oriented toward self-preservation, me-focused
Behavior/ Response Strategies	Help, produce, cooperate, collaborate, problem-solve, mediate, persist	Defend, blame, argue, resist, distract, shut down, avoid difficulties, threaten, overplan, try to please all
Outcome	**Thrive**	**Survive**

Access Your Pathways to Self

How do we cultivate our capacity to remember and lead from Self while we are navigating the daily demands of modern life? We must be deliberate. Building our ability to lead from Self begins with taking a moment to look inside and become self-aware amid action, cultivate our own pathways to rest back into Self, and consciously choose how we wish to engage in any situation.

In many families and cultures, attention is often heavily drawn to *outer* experiences, leaving our internal experience as something we keep to ourselves. This starts from the moment we are born. While success is evaluated by measurable accomplishments, few children have an adult simultaneously guiding them in how to notice and express the inner thoughts and feelings that inevitably arise while engaging in outward action. Instead, a child's inner experience is often disregarded. Adults might say, "Come on. Get over it. Wipe your tears. It's not a big deal." As a result, many of us grew up assuming that emotions were—and perhaps still are—off limits, impossible to understand, and somehow dangerous. We learn to compartmentalize and wall off our inner lives rather than discovering our power to understand, respect, and care for our inner experience. The good news? It's not too late to change this mindset for ourselves and for the students we work with.

With this in mind, let's return to the possibility that living from Self is something we all physically possess and can cultivate. The key to learning how to live with greater Self-leadership is to turn our attention inward, exploring our own pathways to access this state of being: how to find a spark of joy, a moment of peace, a shift in perspective, a remembrance of purpose, an opportunity to relax, or simply acceptance for what is. Through regular practice, we can establish a familiar path back to Self, one that we can follow even in the most trying moments.

The state of Self does not belong to a certain religion, culture, philosophy, or school of thought. Around the world, there are myriad habits, practices, and rituals for individuals and communities that support us in reconnecting (consciously or not) with the experience of Self. The graphic on the next page shows a few examples of practices we and the students we work with can follow as pathways to Self.

As educators focused on helping students access Self more fully, we sometimes jump over what *we* need and how *we* care for our well-being. Given this, take a moment to acknowledge what you already do to connect with Self. What works for you? Many people have their own way of reflecting, decompressing, and centering. Perhaps you take a long walk with your dog, call your sister to tell her about your day, play piano, or write poetry. You may hang out with friends, go to church, or attend an exercise class. When you reflect on how you feel after these activities, you may notice the 8 Cs: a sure sign of being in Self. You can also reflect on the signs that are unique to you, including those you considered at the start of this chapter. The more frequently you invest in resetting your nervous system, the more resilient you will be in the face of stressors.

We may be aware of the things that will reconnect us to Self, but sometimes, the experience of life can be so busy that it seems indulgent or impossible to take time to *do* these things. When we don't prioritize this space for ourselves, it often creates an inner pileup of tension and unresolved experiences. As a result, we may operate with a suboptimal physiology and mindset. Too often days, weeks, and even months seem to pass by and we've taken no time at all to reset. Eventually, we burn out, physically, mentally, and emotionally. Being chronically stressed like this means being consequently less productive. Although it likely seems counterintuitive, often the most efficient thing we can do is discover our unique pathways, giving ourselves brief, regular periods to digest life, integrate our experience, and reconnect with our Self.

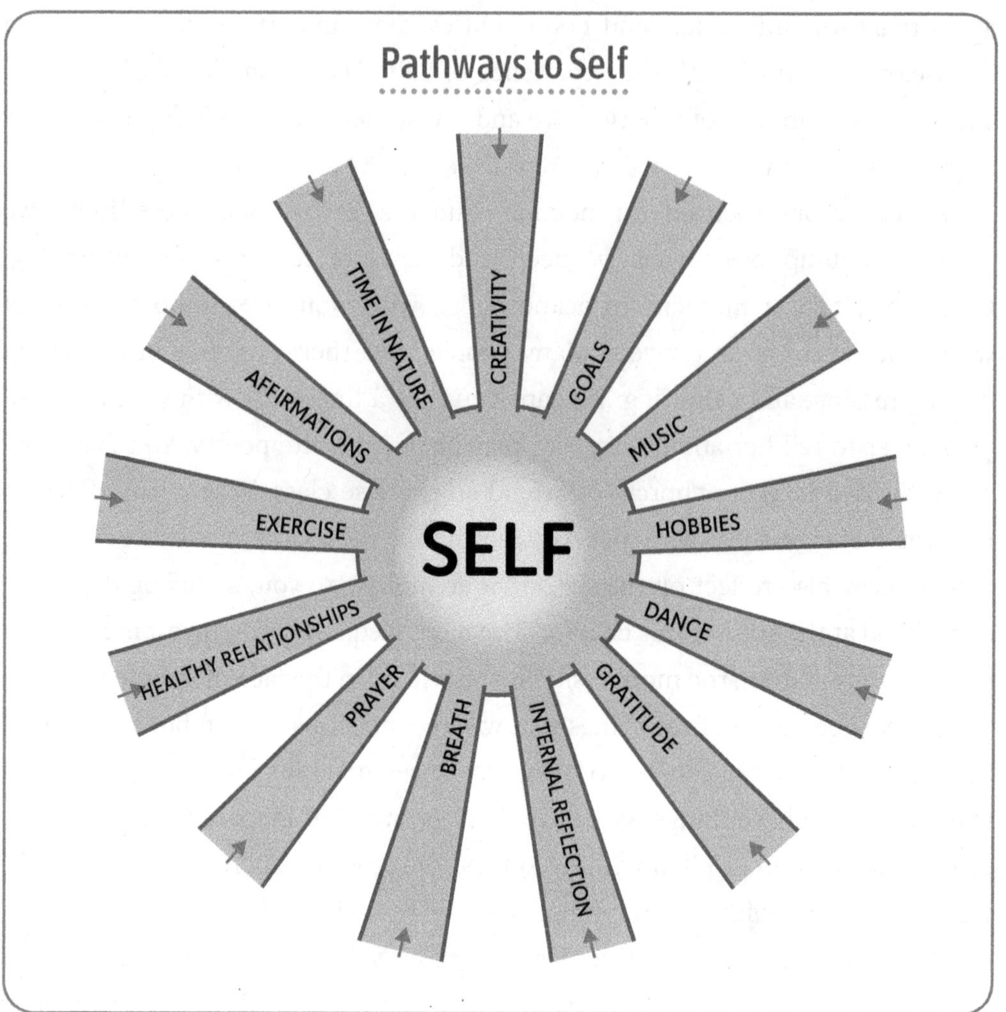

Pause and Reflect

- How do you access the experience of Self?
  - In moments of stress, how do you care for yourself and connect with qualities of Self?
  - What habits or practices help you relax, reflect, or rejuvenate?

The *P* of PAUSE: Pausing to Shift the Moment

Perhaps parts of you are still a bit skeptical about how to find ways to connect with Self. Maybe you've tried self-care or self-reflection but they just feel like one more item on the to-do list. To experience these practices as a *relief*, not a burden, we need simple, bite-size practices that help us reflect, reset, and reconnect in the midst of what we are already doing. What we need are simple ways to *pause*. Recall that pause is the *P* in the PAUSE for Self-Leadership™ model: take a moment to notice what is happening, take a breath, recognize our inner experience, and check our degree of connection to Self. And if this sounds like what we discussed in the previous section, you're right; most of the behaviors on the pathway to Self begin with taking some time, finding a quiet, calm space, or stopping what we're doing to breathe—actions that all take some form of *pausing*.

In schools, many educators intuitively build in moments for students to take a break from the current activity and reset, thus finding pathways to Self. This might look like having circle time in the morning, listening to calming music, or taking a break to walk outside. Similarly, when we are deescalating a student, we start by inviting them to take a breath. More and more schools are creating calm spaces for students to voluntarily visit as they need to self-reflect or self-regulate.

The power of pausing is something many of us already recognize as valuable, even if we struggle to do it. Think about how often we say things like: "I just need to pause and step back"; "When I paused, I realized that what I really wanted to say was . . ."; or "If only I had just taken a moment to pause, it all would have turned out differently."

In just a small amount of time—even just a moment in some cases—we can make meaningful changes to our internal and external worlds. So what makes a pause so powerful? When we pause, we may intuitively:

- Step back and breathe
- Become present to notice and appreciate what is happening around us (i.e., the situation and dynamics)
- Distinguish the external facts from our individual story
- Increase awareness of and acceptance for our inner experience of thoughts, feelings, and sensations

- Create space to calm our body and regulate our nervous system
- Arrive in the present moment, anchoring our attention in sensory details
- Attune to others we are with—their needs, perspective, and state of being
- Gain perspective on what is needed and what is possible
- Return to the big picture and our greater sense of purpose

When we pause, we can use this action to come back to ourselves and remember who we are: our innate good qualities, our capabilities, and the purpose that gives meaning to our effort, even on our hardest days.

Community Application: Pausing

When I began developing the PAUSE for Self-Leadership™ model over a decade years ago, I was working as a school-based community therapist, and my son was in preschool. At the time, many mornings were a juggling act. One particular morning, I was already thinking ahead to what I'd find at work, wondering how I'd respond to depressed students, overwhelmed parents, and frustrated teachers while at the same time trying to escort my three-year-old out the door. Just as I was ready to walk out the door, he was nowhere to be found; I eventually located him hanging upside down off the couch in the living room. I felt exasperated and wanted to react sharply to correct, but I knew this would only create a resistant, crying toddler. I had tried so many strategies on mornings like this—many from parenting books and blogs—and it felt like none of them were working.

That day, I tried shifting my focus *off* my son and back to myself, putting to use what I'd been learning about Self-leadership. I simply stopped moving and stood in the hallway with my coat on, asking myself, *Where am I coming from?* I paused, took a breath, acknowledged my feelings, responses, and all the different parts of me, and then recentered back into Self: How did I want to *be* as a mom? In that moment, I had the power to look at my son with fresh eyes. Wow! I could see a three-year-old boy lost in a moment of delight, wanting to connect and play with his mom and doing the best he could. He was not being difficult, manipulative, or resistant on purpose. I felt as though I could approach him with an open heart, express appreciation for where he was coming from, and gently guide him out the door. Needless to say, this yielded totally different results! Recognizing the profound power of a momentary pause, I started to purposefully practice stepping back to check in with myself. Bit by bit, my capacity to be self-aware and to respond differently grew, and I found the capacity to show up more often as the mom I wanted to be.

Tips to Pause

To learn to pause most effectively, we must practice *on purpose*. Pausing unlocks access to this present moment, the only moment we can live, the only place where we have power to practice how we want to live life. This doesn't mean we need to intentionally put ourselves in stressful situations, but it does mean we need to be deliberate when we do decide—or realize—that it's time to pause. We can pause *proactively*, weaving brief moments into the day to check in with ourselves and recenter in our Selves. We can also pause *responsively*, happening before, during, or after situations or interactions that are stressful. The table on the following page includes some examples of when and how you might practice your pausing using both strategies.

Each time we pause, we step back, breathe, and ask, *What is happening right now both outside me and inside me?* From here, we can gauge if we are relatively connected to Self by looking for the signs of the 8 Cs. If we measure that we are stressed and *not* in Self, we can use a brief strategy to reset our nervous system (see the list of suggested pause practices on the next page). As we make pausing a regular practice, we grow our self-awareness and our ability to respond more effectively in the moment.

Pausing Practices

Pausing Proactively	Pausing Responsively
• Pause in the morning before starting work, remembering how you want to be amid all you do. Remember your why: your purpose that gives meaning to your work. • Put a sticky note with a reminder, key word, or action on your computer or in your office at work. Some examples might be *Breathe*, *Be present*, or *Be curious*. • Pause when you walk in and out of the door of your classroom or office and enjoy one conscious breath. Look around and see the space you are in. • Pause between meetings and tasks to easefully transition. Give yourself a minute to make a cup of tea, walk down the hallway, or look out the window. • Pause as you drive home. No phone calls. No music. Just check in with yourself. As if talking to your best friend, ask yourself, *How are you?* • Give yourself a regular inner pause through contemplative and meditative practices. Build in deeper pauses, which can be dedicated times each week to unplug, reflect, and reset your nervous system.	• Pause when you notice a physical stress response. Witness the sensations, such as heart racing, tension, or shallow breathing. Invite your breath to deepen and your body to soften, regulating your nervous system. • Pause when you recognize an automatic instinct to react. Step back and choose not to act just yet. Check in with the thoughts and feelings driving you. Reconnect with how you want to respond and choose the best action to take next. • Pause in interactions, inviting others to stop action with you for a moment to breathe and reflect. • Pause with small groups, or even a class full of students, by following a brief recorded inner reflection practice. Not only do you get a minute for yourself, but the whole group can downshift together as well. • Pause before or after a triggering conversation to calm your body, acknowledge your feelings, and attend to your needs. Consider how you can be purposeful moving forward.

Reflective Pause Practice: Proactive, Sustained Self-Care

Thus far, we've considered the value in identifying our natural pathways to Self and the power of simply pausing in the midst of our busy days. To build our capacity and awareness to lead from Self, it's helpful to engage in reflective pause practices to intentionally shift our attention to our inner experience for a designated period of time. This can take the form of contemplation, prayer, or meditation. Over time, we will increase our familiarity with our inner world and develop a conscious and compassionate relationship with ourselves. As we attend to our own inner landscape, we practice witnessing, without judgment, the inner conversation of thoughts, feelings, voices, stories, wishes, and worries that typically run on autopilot, unconsciously coloring our experience and driving our lives. We increase our attunement to the signals our system is sending us all day: signs of stress and signs of Self. This very practice of witnessing our inner life often facilitates a physiological shift in the moment: We rest back into Self. It allows us to unhook from the running inner narrative, the floods of emotions, and the physical hijacks, and gain perspective.

Reflective practices also afford a space to intentionally focus on Self and practice remembrance of the 8 Cs, our values, our capacity, and our purpose. Additionally, we can practice gratitude and appreciate all we have—the good people that surround us and our current opportunities and resources. Reflective practices connect us to our power and put our system at ease, recognizing we are an adult that can handle life. They support us in approaching our day from a clear and centered space. This is more enjoyable for us and leads to more productive, beneficial results.

Here are a few brief practices to pause and keep company with your inner experience. As you read them, feel free to try them right now:

- **Focus on your breath:** Without judging or changing it, just notice the flow of your breath in this moment, as it is. The breath is flowing easefully in and out of your body on its own. At the end of each inhale and exhale, there is a momentary pause. Now, for three breaths, rest your attention on the natural rhythm: receiving breath in, pausing, releasing breath out, pausing. Notice any effect.

- **Focus on physical sensations:** Scan through your body, noticing sensations of warmth or cold, tension or relaxation, energy or tiredness. Be curious and accepting as you discover each different sensation. Without judging what you find as good or bad, simply accept it as it is, opening yourself to the feeling of being alive in this moment. Keeping company with yourself in this way, remind yourself that right now, right here, in this moment, everything is okay. Value your experience.
- **Focus on thoughts and feelings:** Focus inside and notice what thoughts or feelings come to your attention. One by one, notice and name them. "Oh, I am thinking about going grocery shopping." Got it. What else is there? "I see I am trying to figure out that situation at work." Noted. What else is there? "I sense a tightness in my chest with a feeling of some worry . . . not sure what about." In this way, you hear and sense your inner dialogue and inner activity. As you do this, you build a familiarity and even a friendship with yourself on the inside. You also experience a little space from the intensity of inner activity and in this, regain some poise and choice.
- **Focus on one of the 8 Cs:** Activate your Self detector. Scan the list of the 8 Cs and look for one quality that you are experiencing right now, even a little bit: calm, compassion, courage, curiosity, confidence, clarity, creativity, or connection. Appreciate that you possess this quality. Rest your attention on how you experience it in this moment. Now breathe into it, letting it slowly expand within you like a balloon, starting from your center and spreading out to your extremities. You may repeat to yourself, "I am [*C quality*]." Do this for one minute. Then, be aware of the effect. Consider if you now have more access to another of the C qualities.

What did you discover in these few exercises? People are often amazed at the degree of shift that can occur when they only take a few minutes to pause. Our mind is a powerful tool. While there are many external stressors and real factors influencing our day-to-day lives, we have much more power over our experience than we realize. Through reflective practices, the space emerges to differentiate the various elements of our inner experience, like unraveling a ball of yarn. We become familiar with the cycles and patterns of thoughts and feelings that unconsciously drive our lives. As we bring these patterns into awareness, we have the opportunity to know and attend to ourselves as we would a dear friend, bringing our curiosity and kindness to appreciate ourselves *as we are*. With a greater sense of harmony inside, we can return to building greater harmony with all that is outside.

Conclusion

Practicing pausing and inner reflective practices are not things that you *should* do. Rather, I offer these exercises as invitations to know and befriend yourself. They're not about stopping the mind, controlling our feelings, judging our experience, or managing negative impulses. It's actually quite the opposite. Our goal is to relate to our own selves with compassion, curiosity, and acceptance. We become familiar with the wise signals our inner system offers us. We grow attuned to what supports us to access and act from Self. We open to the possibility to experience greater ease, clarity, and even joy as we move through our days. It is a gift we can give ourselves.

The more we check in with ourselves, coming back to our center, the more power we have to live with Self-leadership. As we make time and space to reset daily, we establish a new inner baseline, a foundation for well-being. This helps prepare us for rough moments when our stress response is activated. As we practice looking inward, we can recognize the signals earlier and travel back to center more easily. The time we invest in focused practice transforms our capacity to show up present and engaged amid the dynamics of everyday life. As we attend to our own self-discovery, we build our knowledge and skill to guide our students to do the same.

Stories from the Field

Listening and Connecting to Self Helps Me Teach

Craig Lundell is an audio engineering teacher at an urban technical high school in Connecticut.

When I started teaching, I had no formal training in classroom management or social-emotional learning. I left my industry career to teach trade technology at a city high school; I came into the school midyear. I was eager to train students to become professional audio engineers; however, I found that some of the students were disrespectful to me and refused to participate in class. Knowing that this kind of behavior would result in their termination from any professional job in the field, I pushed back hard. Instead of earning the respect of my students, I ended up engaged in power struggles resulting in disciplinary actions. When a student refused to work on an assignment, I became frustrated and fixated on their behavior. I would hover until they either started to work or I had to escalate. I found myself saying, "You can't just sit here in my classroom and not do any work. Get started or I'll have to send you out. Your choice."

I did not realize that my brain was basically running an algorithm: If this student does A, then I escalate to B. I was so caught up in this struggle that I lost sight of my goal—to teach students a trade technology that they could use to gain employment after graduation (and even more, to support them to build the essential skills for success, such as self-awareness, resilience, collaboration). I had no idea that my behavior was impacting the behavior of my students and I didn't have perspective on why the students were behaving the way they were.

When I began my Self-leadership training, I really liked what I was hearing, but I did not realize how powerful it could be until I started to try it out. I began to shift my focus from my students to myself, noticing how I was acting and becoming conscious of the moments when I was triggered. Now that I use a Self-led approach, I can see what is happening in the moment. Instead of escalating the situation, I take a moment to pause and refocus on my goal: student learning and well-being. I have discovered that there are all kinds of reasons that a student might behave in a disruptive way; students are often consumed by very real concerns about family, friends, poverty, or other issues. I learned how to connect when a student became off-task and begin a conversation about what is really going on. Now that I am coming from a more peaceful and Self-led place, my students are much more likely to be open to working with me and to make a plan that gets them reengaged. In more extreme instances, I can now recognize when they really need to talk to a counselor (versus my past pattern of sending them to an administrator). My Self-led behavior earns the respect of my students and has a positive effect on my classroom environment. Now I am more ready to teach and the students are more ready to learn.

Invitations to Practice

 REFLECT: *Layers of Experience*

Begin by finding an easy posture and shift your attention to your inner experience. Settle into the layers of your experience. Start by noticing your *physical experience*. Acknowledge physical signs, like tension, temperature, energy, or numbness. See if you can hold just a little curiosity or compassion in relationship to your body. Breathe.

Now, place your attention on your *thoughts*. Notice what's on your mind; perhaps you are debriefing an event, planning for the future, or processing an experience. Acknowledge the effort your mind is making on your behalf. Offer your mind the spirit of compassion. Breathe.

Now notice the levels of *feelings* within you. Acknowledge them. See if you can offer them the spirit of curiosity. Breathe.

Finally, settle your attention on your *core*, where the breath is traveling in and out of you, easily and naturally. Rest here in the space of the breath. If your attention wanders to the layers of feelings, thoughts, or sensations, that is fine. Notice when this happens, offer your compassion to these parts of you, and then rest back in the breath.

EMBODY: *Sensing the Present Moment Walk*

Take a short walk outside, experimenting with anchoring your attention in the present moment. Your senses can be a doorway. What do you see? What do you smell? What do you hear? What do you feel? Notice the details you see, like colors, shapes, movement, temperature, and the wind. Notice the objects and their details as if you are experiencing them for the first time. When you notice that you are distracted, gently refocus on the present moment. At the end of your walk, take stock of your inner experience and note any shift toward signs of Self, such as feeling more calm, more clear, or more connected.

WRITE: *Signs of Self*

Take a few moments to reflect on your inner experience and notice the ways you are currently experiencing (or not experiencing) signs of Self. The 8 Cs can serve as your portal. Self-assess how much (or how little) you are experiencing each of the Cs. You may notice what contributes to your state of being or what takes you toward Self versus away from it. Be an inner explorer, building self-awareness. As you do this, focus on observing, not judging.

____

____

____

____

____

____

____

____

____

ACT: *Shifts During the Day*

As you move through your day, take brief micropauses to notice any signs that you might be in a state of stress versus in Self. If you are not in Self, consider what you might need to reset or shift in the moment. Experiment with what works: perhaps taking a breath, adjusting your posture, or looking out a window. How do you shift from stress to Self?

CHAPTER 2

Aware of Yourself: Befriending Your Inner Team

Pause and Reflect

- As you move through the school day, what different parts of you surface in challenging moments?
  - What happens inside you when you are running late?
  - What sides of you come up when learning a new skill?
- How about with students?
  - What is your instinctual response when a student is resistant, shuts down, or overreacts?

In challenging situations, numerous reactions can overtake us. As we've discussed, there are many quick and easy ways to pause, reset, and recenter. And then there are those moments when no matter how hard we try to stay calm and manage our response, we are hijacked by a knee-jerk reaction. Not being in the driver's seat of our own lives can be mystifying, frustrating, exhausting, and discouraging. As educators, we may also be baffled by students, wondering what is happening when they don't seem to have control over their behavior and emotions. We might think, *I'm using everything in my toolbox, but nothing is working. I'm giving clear instructions, patiently adapting to my students' needs, but still, their buttons get pushed—a switch flips and suddenly they are irrational and extreme. Then I'm activated too and can barely hold it together! What's happening? What can I do?*

In these moments, for both the teacher and the students, it may seem almost impossible to access or even remember the capacity to act from Self. What if we could understand these powerful and mysterious inner dynamics and have an effective way to relate to ourselves and others?

In the first chapter, we established a recognition of our different states: when we are in a stress response and self-protective versus when we are more Self-led. We also explored our power to pause, become self-aware, and purposefully shift. This chapter will delve further into what happens inside us during these stress-filled "takeover" moments, and then learn how we can best care for ourselves.

In this chapter, we will:

- Explore the possibility that we all have multiple parts and learn how this explains our more extreme reactions
- Build awareness of parts (in ourselves and others) so we can better "see" what is happening
- Learn to be the leader of our internal system of parts
- Experience how to relate to our parts effectively to support regulation, self-compassion, and productive engagement

We All Have Parts

Hearing this idea that you have parts may activate feelings of excitement and curiosity as well as discomfort or skepticism. Appreciating these responses, consider how, in your everyday life, you probably run into emotions and reactions in others that derail situations and perhaps aggravate you. You probably also have to navigate the ups and downs of your own moods and reactions; some days go smoothly and some are rough. Thinking of these experiences in terms of parts can help you see what's happening inside and make sense of the confusing and contradictory reactions you sometimes experience in yourself and others.

"When I first heard we were going to discuss our parts and look inside, I was like, *I don't think so*. However, I was curious. As the workshop on Self-leadership proceeded, I was increasingly intrigued by the idea that I might have my own parts that were begging to be seen and understood. I kept wondering if a better understanding of my parts might help me be more curious about the challenging behaviors I was seeing in my students.

To say understanding parts, both mine and my students', has been a game changer is an understatement. While there were times when student dysregulation made me deeply uncomfortable, I found relief and a sense of choice in those intense moments. Instead of becoming unglued, I have the tools to remain in Self and take action with curiosity and compassion."

—**Dr. Melissa Zych,** music teacher, Title I public school, Connecticut

The Development of Parts

In the IFS model, *parts* are understood as the distinct sides or aspects of our personality. To better appreciate how parts operate, let's consider how they develop and take on their role in our inner systems. As we discussed in chapter 1, we each have our unique go-to responses to life's challenges and stresses—some more Self-led and some more self-protective. But what is the origin of our unique response strategies?

From the day we are born, we are tasked with figuring out how to survive. Along with our fundamental needs for food, shelter, and safety, we also need to be seen, included, and valued. We need to know we matter. To meet these needs, we search for connection and belonging with our caregivers, experimenting with different strategies to seek and gain these benefits. For example, we may cry when we are lonely, act cute when we want something, have a tantrum when we don't get something, behave well to receive praise, or anticipate others' needs to please them. As we test various approaches, we see what response they elicit from adults: Do we get eye contact, engagement, reassurance, or company? Are we included and valuable to our family or community? Are we brought in closer or pushed away? Through trial and error, one interaction at a time, we collect information about what works, taking on different beliefs and assumptions about ourselves and the world.

As we grow up, we put our research to the test: When faced with what appears to be a familiar stressor, our "tried and tested" response rises up. This response isn't only a thought, feeling, or behavior, but a bundled response: a practiced *combination* of thoughts, feelings, and behaviors that are wired together. We've encoded and stored our learned responses at every level of our system. In IFS, these are what we refer to as our *parts*. The following image shows some of the ways we might experience these parts.

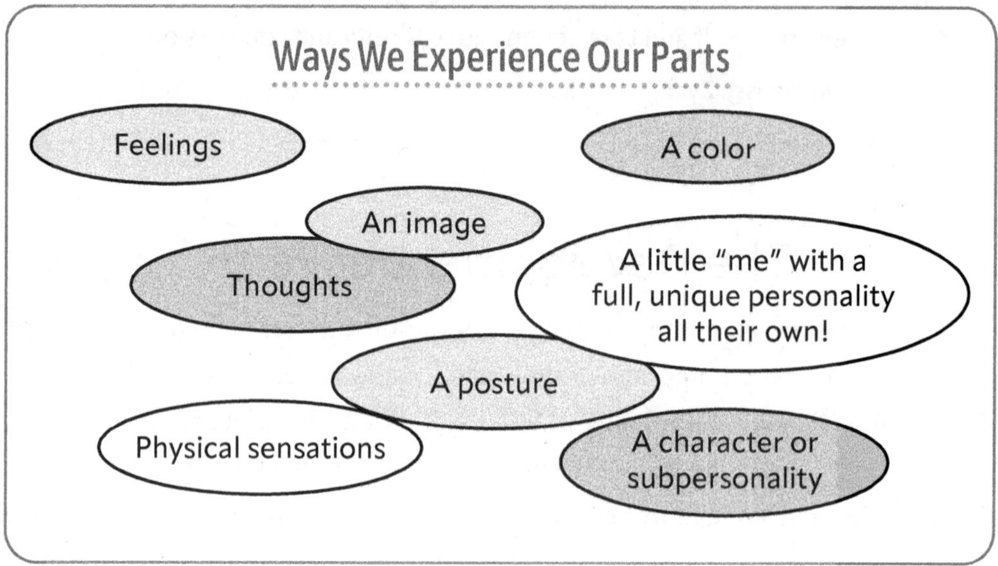

We develop our parts in the context of our everyday relationship with our caregivers. When we can rely on our caregivers to provide a secure connection, we are able to learn, take risks, and develop autonomy and competence. This will cultivate parts of us that feel courageous, calm, and confident—in other words, parts that operate with qualities of Self-leadership. In moments when our caregivers are not available, responsive, and attuned, we will experience stress and cultivate more self-protective parts that will do anything necessary to feel safe. Through our life experience, our response strategies evolve as a *team* of parts, taking on different traits and roles unique to our experience. It is in the container of these childhood relationships that we develop our sense of identity, our understanding of relationships, and our blueprint for learning.

Our Experience of Parts

We all experience various parts of ourselves all day, whether we are aware of it or not. We may notice their presence when they surface as shifts in our emotions and moods. Parts show up as the conversation between different voices in our head or the different sides of ourselves that we display in the course of a day. Sometimes we recognize parts through a change in our physical state, like the weight of the world on our shoulders or a pit in our stomach. Other times, we identify our parts when we feel like we are wearing a mask, such as putting on our best game face at school, even when we feel crummy inside.

We often speak of our parts using various terms such as character traits or sides of ourselves. We even have phrases that reference our different parts: "My buttons got pushed," "I felt hijacked," "That was a different side of me," or even, "Right now part of me thinks I should do one thing, but another part of me thinks something else." All these examples reflect different ways we intuitively recognize the natural multiplicity of our mind. The following image shows some of the other names we might use in our everyday language to describe our parts.

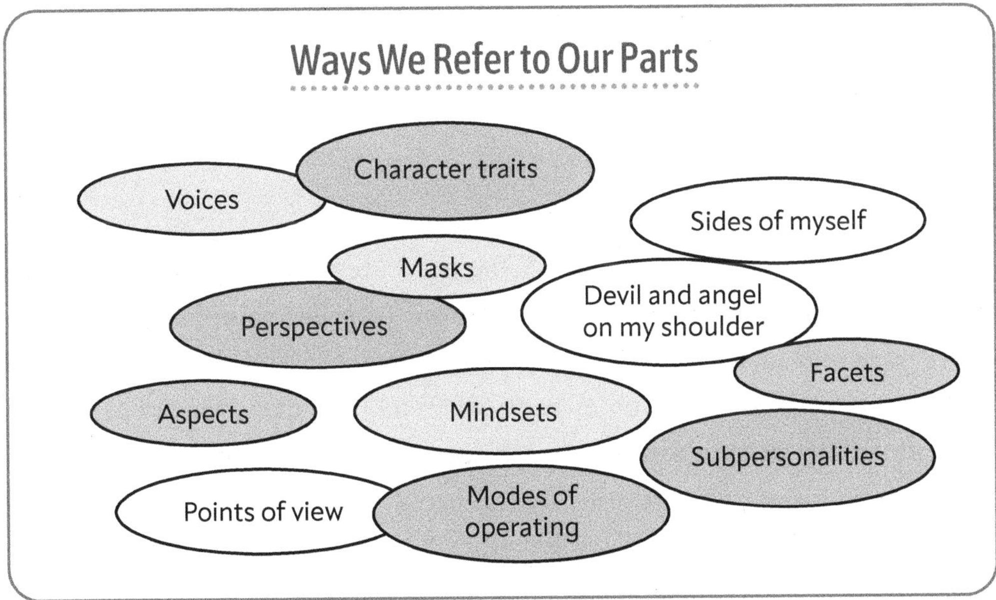

Parts are innate from birth, and they evolve in response to our lived experience to help us navigate the myriad circumstances and relationships we encounter each day. Consider the many parts of you that juggle your daily life. For example, you may have a part that listens attentively to a friend, another part that helps organize your responsibilities, and another part that's needed to lead a group of children. You may also have parts that get frustrated when others don't follow directions, are controlling when things are disorganized, or withdraw when you feel misunderstood.

It's important to note that parts are not good or bad. They each have their own unique function and personalities, including needs, preferences, and opinions. Ideally, they work toward their goal in harmony with other parts, taking turns and responding in ways that are beneficial for us and the situation. When our inner team of parts follows our lead, we have Self-leadership.

Each part believes it is fulfilling a role, helping us stay safe and get our needs met. We can consider that all our parts took on their roles because at some point in time, it seemed like the best way to cope and, sometimes, to survive. Because of this, all parts have a positive intent, and IFS invites us to try on the attitude of respecting and welcoming all parts. In fact, as we start to notice different parts of us rise and subside in the course of our experience we can try on the following understanding from IFS: "All parts are welcome." With this attitude, we can see how this can shift our perception of and relationship with ourselves. (It's important to note that we can welcome our parts while not necessarily endorsing their associated behaviors and impact.)

Our Unique Parts

Most of us like some parts of ourselves and are not fond of others. There might even be some we downright dislike. Some parts seem to be counterproductive; they may act in extreme ways, shut us down, or even cause harm to others. These parts took on a role to protect us at some point in the *past* and are now on autopilot, not realizing that times have changed. They may even act as though they are frozen in another time and place. For example, consider a student who grew up living with a volatile, critical parent. A part of this child may have taken on intense beliefs such as "Something's wrong with me." They may use more extreme protective strategies, such as yelling, to defend themselves. Five years later in school, that part may rise up automatically, the child yelling at their teacher in response to reasonable feedback. The yelling seems childish and disproportional to the situation, but it is understandable when we consider it as a part with a positive intent based on past experience.

Because our parts develop in response to our unique life experiences as a strategy to meet our needs and protect us, everybody's parts are different. One person's anxious part may have a different origin and agenda than another person's anxious part. Moreover, there is no fixed number of parts for each person. IFS offers a framework to recognize, understand, and connect with our unique parts. As we begin to see and understand ourselves in this new way, we can become an expert caregiver for our own inner experience.

As you start to understand the idea of parts, you may notice and wonder about your own parts and how they may have been formed. You may even have parts of you bubbling up as you read this chapter. If this happens, I invite you to keep a list for yourself of the different parts you detect. You can think of these as *trailheads* for your inner journey. Later in this chapter, we will cover a simple, safe method to get to know your parts and honor them while increasing your experience of Self-leadership.

A Family of Parts: The Inner System

We each have a whole team or family of parts inside of us. Different parts step up and take over at different times. If we look inside ourselves and track our different parts over a period of time, we will start to notice patterns of interaction among them. Schwartz (2020), who originally identified this understanding of parts, first recognized these patterns of interaction in his work with clients who had eating disorders. Schwartz's clients weren't responding to the latest models and tools for family therapy, so he gave up his agenda and instead asked his clients to describe their inner experience; they described an inner conversation of different voices that went something like this:

- One part was judgmental and critical of the client's weight and told them to stop eating.
- Eventually, in reaction to this unbearable restraint, another part took over and began to seek relief, driving them to binge eat.
- In turn, this behavior activated underlying parts that carried feelings of shame and worthlessness.
- Finally, this triggered the original part to reinstate strict management of food intake.

Just like the dynamics of interaction within a family, this internal family of parts had a different role they worked hard to fulfill and were responding in reaction to each other, much like we see in family systems. Additionally, Schwartz found that through these patterns of interaction, the parts are continually striving to reestablish a sense of relief or being okay. While parts were often at odds with each other, like a group of quarreling siblings, Schwartz found that parts also responded powerfully when he supported his clients to enter into dialogue with their parts in a Self-led way, with curiosity and compassion. He found he could guide clients to act as their own inner leader, the inner parent that the parts needed to bring ease and harmony within. In other words, the principles of human systems that are relevant to interpersonal relationships could also be applied to the internal systems of parts.

Schwartz soon confirmed that it was not only clients with eating disorders, or even people grappling with mental illness, who experienced parts. As Schwartz and his colleagues tested their model with people around the world, they found that we all have this inner family of parts continually interacting with and counterbalancing each other. The key is to get to know these inner parts: who they are, how they interact with each other, and how these interactions drive our lives. Just as educators take time to get to know each of their students and notice the dynamics in their class community, we too can familiarize ourselves with our inner community of parts. We can learn to recognize parts that are in a healthy state of balance while also lovingly attending to those that have assumed more extreme and protective roles. From a place of Self-leadership, we can connect with our parts and work with them to validate, regulate, and provide for them in healthy ways, simultaneously contributing to the whole inner family system. As educators, we can use this technique to lead our own parts as well as to coach young people in doing the same for themselves.

Three Types of Parts

Although we have our own unique team of parts, each individual part falls into one of three distinct categories based on the role they play in the inner system. IFS calls these categories *exiles*, *managers*, and *firefighters*. (IFS also refers to the latter two categories as *protectors.*) We will unpack these different types of parts individually, and then we will explore how they behave in relationship to one another as a system. As we do this, consider how you see these different types of parts in your students, your colleagues, and yourself.

Exiles: Vulnerable Parts

When we come into this world, we possess our core Self and a team of parts that are essentially valuable and full of potential. These parts are curious to learn, eager to connect, excited to discover, and in search of comfort. Each of them works to get our basic needs met. But no matter how attentive our caregivers are, there are times, especially when we are young, when our needs are not met in some way. In these moments, we feel and believe that we are vulnerable, alone, scared, out of control, or not good enough. Needless to say, we don't like the experience of these vulnerable feelings, and we often get a clear signal they are not welcomed by others.

Thus, our inner system conspires to push these parts down, hide them, and banish them into the basement of our consciousness. Not surprisingly, these parts are referred to as *exiles*. They remain under the surface but are inevitably activated over the course of the day. The following graphic shows some of the thoughts and beliefs our exiles might hold.

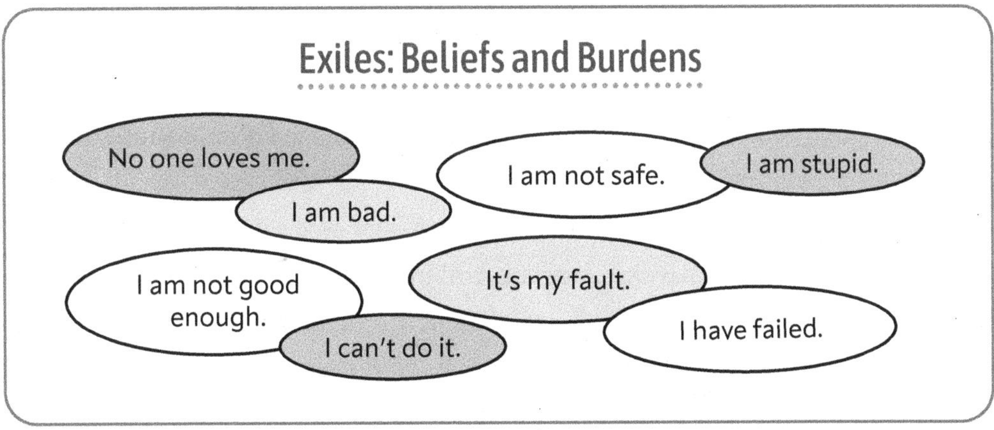

In school, we may see exiles pop up when students are confronted with new academic material or an unpredictable social situation that triggers a sense of vulnerability. As adults, we might experience an exile, if only briefly, when we feel misunderstood or unappreciated, or if we believe we've failed on the job. We might sense it as a sort of emptiness, a weight in our chest, a wave of fear, or an underlying restlessness.

Even as you read this, you may recognize how you experience your exiles. If so, keep in mind that this is probably a young part of you that, in the simplest sense, just needs loving attention. Later in this chapter, you will learn more about how to care for and relate to these parts.

Protectors: Managers and Firefighters

Managers and firefighters are two different types of parts that protect us from experiencing the energy of our exile parts. The protector's motto is *Never again*. As you can imagine, the more trauma we've experienced (and the more vulnerability and shame we've been exposed to), the harder our protectors will work to make sure the bad things in our past never happen to us again.

There are two strategies for protectors. The manager's job is to be *proactive*; they anticipate and prevent the exiled feelings from coming up or getting out, keeping them contained. The firefighter's role is *reactive*; they douse the "flames" of the exiled feelings when the exiles do manage to escape the manager's preventive measures. Let's look a bit more closely at these two protective parts.

MANAGERS

Managers are preemptive and proactive. They try to anticipate what could go wrong and what might activate the exiled part. They often focus on being good and doing good to avoid feeling bad. The following image shows some examples of manager behaviors.

Generally, our society likes and rewards manager parts. They are perceived as "good" and are often socially appropriate, driving us to be who we "should" be. In moderation, and when Self-led, a certain amount of manager energy is needed to navigate daily life. However, we often fail to recognize how burdened these parts can be, working so hard to be perfect, please everyone, and keep things under control 24/7.

Manager parts can easily feel burdened in the context of our schools. Students' manager parts work to be compliant, focused, productive, and liked by others, sometimes to the extreme. Educators' manager parts may show up as caregivers, planners, and disciplinarians. Although motivated to ensure students have care and structure, these parts can drive us to extremes—on the one hand, sometimes overreacting, and on the other hand, focusing on others at the expense of our own well-being. As a result, we may end up living a good portion of our days in a manager mode that is exhausting, frustrating, and unfulfilling. In spite of knowing this, we often don't see another way to be. (We will get to this soon!)

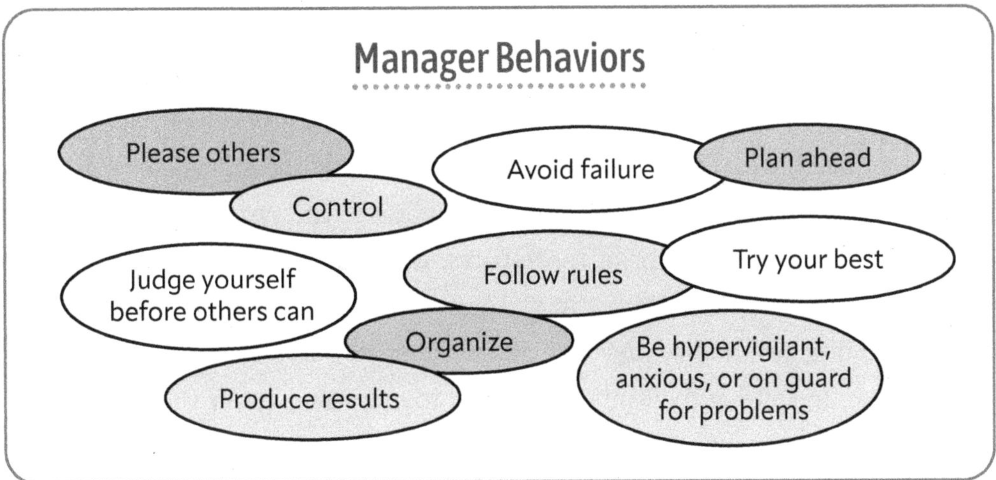

FIREFIGHTERS

Though our manager parts aim to be extremely vigilant, there are still moments when the exiles and their associated feelings escape. When we detect the exiles' energy, we often need some sort of quick relief in order to feel good again. This is when *firefighters* come to the rescue, in full reactive and "extinguishing" mode. These parts help to quickly avoid, escape, or distract from the perceived threat of an exile takeover. Here's the catch: The relief is temporary. Afterward, we generally experience the shame of exiles again, sometimes even more strongly due to our behavior while in firefighter mode. As with all parts, firefighters can present on a spectrum from moderate pleasures to extreme addictions. The following image shows some of the more common firefighter behaviors.

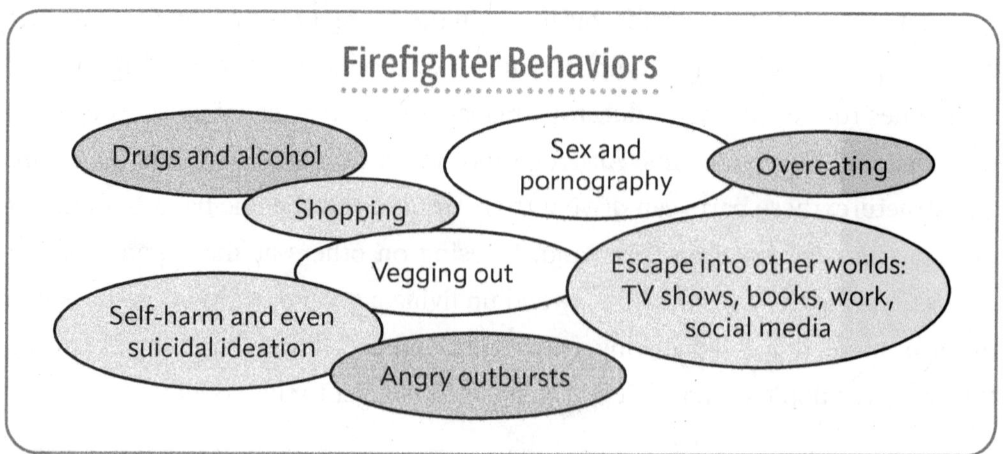

The general message about firefighters in our society is that their behaviors are bad. We are often taught that we shouldn't engage in these behaviors, and if we get into bad habits because of firefighters, we should overcome—or *manage*—them. Though their actions may seem detrimental to the system, we often don't appreciate the positive intent of these parts. From their point of view, they are superheroes, coming in to save the system when no one else is there to do it. Like a true first responder, they will do anything to give us relief from the pain of our exiles. In spite of their intent, we tend to judge and attack them right after they try to help. A manager part will say to a firefighter, "What were you thinking eating a whole pint of ice cream? That's terrible. Get it together!" However, this judgment only energizes firefighters to dig their heels in deeper and thus, the inner battle commences! What we don't realize is that once we acknowledge firefighters for their positive intent, they are often more than happy to help us find alternative ways to get our needs met—they just want us to feel relief.

A few firefighter parts we see in students include excessively escaping to content on screens and devices, overconsuming junk food, playing class clown, refusing to engage, and experiencing emotional eruptions. When we see firefighter parts in school, we can understand that it is coming up in reaction to a student's exile being triggered. If we can reserve judgment and discover what happened before the firefighter came on the scene, we can likely identify what called them to duty. We may experience our firefighter parts as wanting to ignore a student's disruptive behavior, slipping out for a donut in the faculty lounge, or sipping several glasses of wine in the evening while scrolling social media. Of course, much of this behavior is normal and understandable, and in moderation, it isn't an issue. However, if the exile's pain is intense enough, firefighter parts' behavior can become off-balance, and even harmful. In any event, firefighter behaviors tend to prevent us from getting what we really want, which is lasting relief for our exile's pain.

Common Protectors

Because parts develop in response to our unique life experiences, we each have our distinct, customized team of parts, but there are many parts we may have in common. The following list shows just a few. As you review this list of parts, consider which ones you are familiar with from life at school: Which of these parts do you see present in students, adults, and even yourself? Can you tell which are managers (preemptive) and which are firefighters (reactive)?

- **Anticipator:** Predicts criticism, problems, and bad things, and tries to preempt them
- **Binger:** Distracts by absorbing your attention into something—like food, social media, or alcohol—that gives you a time-limited "high"
- **Boss:** Wants everything perfectly organized and under control so there isn't any chaos
- **Clown:** Is always the life of the party, distracting you from what is unhappy or stressful
- **Couch potato:** Is lazy and spacey to avoid life's stresses and demands
- **Critic:** Notices everything it thinks you do wrong and criticizes you before others can
- **Dragon:** Blames and burns others when things go wrong to relieve you from considering your part or feeling your fear
- **Eeyore (from *Winnie the Pooh*):** Expects the worst so you won't be disappointed
- **Escape artist:** Quickly runs from the scene when relationships or situations become challenging
- **Fog:** Feels fuzzy-minded, depressed, and tired to protect you from fully feeling and engaging with the intensity of life

- **Game face:** Always appears put together, in control, professional, and successful
- **Knight in shining armor:** Is always strong, valiant, and powerful, saving the day so people will admire you
- **Mama/Papa Bear:** Closely watches and protects to keep others safe, covering underlying fears or sense of inadequacy
- **Overthinker:** Ruminates over options and issues trying to get it right, always worried about making a wrong choice and looking stupid
- **Pleaser:** Predicts what people want and does everything possible to make them happy
- **Procrastinator:** Anticipating pain or discomfort, avoids what needs to get done
- **Relentless:** Believes that if they keep saying or doing the same thing over and over, their needs will finally be understood and met
- **Reticent/muzzle:** Holds back thoughts and is reluctant to speak up to prevent embarrassment or conflict
- **Sharp intellect:** Steps in to figure out, rationalize, and explain, especially when uncomfortable or confusing feelings surface
- **Superhero:** Selflessly helps in every situation to prove you are good and worthy
- **Wall:** Separates feelings from mind, acts tough and strong, blocking discomfort

Blending: When Parts Take Over

By now, you can probably recall times when your parts, whether manager, firefighter, or exile, have taken over. We all know these moments well. We are flooded. There is a total shift in our physiological state. Our mind races. We are overwhelmed with emotions. We may feel we can't control our words and actions. In these situations, we are *blended* with a part; this is who we believe we are in the moment.

As we cultivate attunement to our unique signs of stress, we can recognize when we are blended with a part. When we learn to notice this blending, we can breathe, step back, and recognize the part of us is just that—a *part* (not all of who we are). When this happens, we *unblend* and can be with the experience of our part but not identify with it completely.

By remembering that a part is not the whole of who we are, we can bring greater self-compassion in moments when we are blended with a part. We are not an angry/anxious/indulgent/depressed person; rather, a part of us is angry/anxious/indulging/feeling depressed. In addition, we must remember that the actions of a blended part are a strategy to avoid feeling an exile's energy and emotions. As we work with others, especially students, we can operate with the conviction that no matter how intense their emotions or how intractable their behavior appears, their parts simply want what is best for them. Furthermore, we are all more than the parts we are blended with at any given moment.

Understanding Our Team of Parts

As you learned in the last section, we each have our own unique inner team of parts, each playing roles in relationship to each other. Some parts are more protective, interacting as managers, firefighters, and exiles, while other parts are more Self-led. As our parts play out the roles and dynamics they have rehearsed throughout our lives, we may continue to feel at war within, overtaken by the ebb and flow of emotions, and out of control. All of our parts ultimately want what is best for us, and in trying to help, they will respond when they experience inner leadership that respects them. When we unblend from our parts and relate to them as we would a person, they respond. That's right. And as we build a connection with one part at a time, they will follow our leadership and even work together for the good of the whole.

Parts will deescalate, cooperate, and even change roles when they trust us. This possibility only emerges when we access Self and internally relate to our parts with genuine compassion and curiosity. To more fully appreciate how to bring Self-leadership to our inner system of parts, let's closely consider the various dynamics at play within.

Polarized Parts

We often find two of our parts going head-to-head with opposite agendas. For example, we have one part that wants a strict exercise schedule and another part that wants to go with the flow and watch TV on the couch. We have a part that says we should finish grading papers and a part that wants to play with our own children when we finally get home. These polarizations are often the tension between a manager and a firefighter. This can be experienced as a sort of "war" in our head. These polarizations also help us explain why decision-making and personal change can be hard.

In the school context, educators are often puzzled by students who commit to renew their efforts or change their attitude, only to slip into disruptive or counterproductive behaviors within minutes. This is a case of polarized parts: One part wants to change and another part wants the comfort or safety of the status quo. Acknowledging the positive intent of both parts allows us to send a message of understanding, allowing the parts to relax and trust us. We aren't trying to control them, and we are not treating one as good and one as bad. It is possible, then, to explore the underlying needs for both parts and mediate toward lasting solutions (just like we would with two children in conflict). We might say something like "I understand that right now one part of you feels ____ and at the same time another part of you needs ____. It seems to me that both sides have an understandable perspective (or need)." This generally allows both parts to step back from their polarization and make space to consider a unifying question: "What might work for both parts of you?"

Most of us can recognize parts of ourselves that sometimes get cranked up too high. As we become familiar with our parts and learn to lead from Self, we can regulate their intensity. When we speak internally to our planner part, we might say, "Thank you for helping me to plan ahead. I am well-prepared and I am content with what I have done. Can you dial it down and give me a little space? I've got this!" When we speak to a student who exhibits anxious or controlling behavior, we could say something similar: "I see a part of you working really hard to plan ahead. It looks like you are well-prepared. Perhaps you could invite that planner part of you to dial back a little now. How would that be for you?" (Note that in this example, we do not pathologize or label by saying, "You are anxious.")

Parts on a Continuum

We all have a range of parts, some more Self-led and some more protective, but like us, they do not operate at the same level every single day. One part may manifest in a more regulated way one day and in a more extreme way the next, as if on a spectrum. For example, being diligent to plan ahead can be a responsible trait, but when it's cranked up from a 5 to a 10, this responsible part of us can feel excessive or intense if we feel the need to organize perfectly or schedule every minute of the day. The following image shows a visual representation of this continuum. Though the same external stressor may cause a Self-led or self-protective response, the corresponding behaviors of the part can occur anywhere along a wide spectrum.

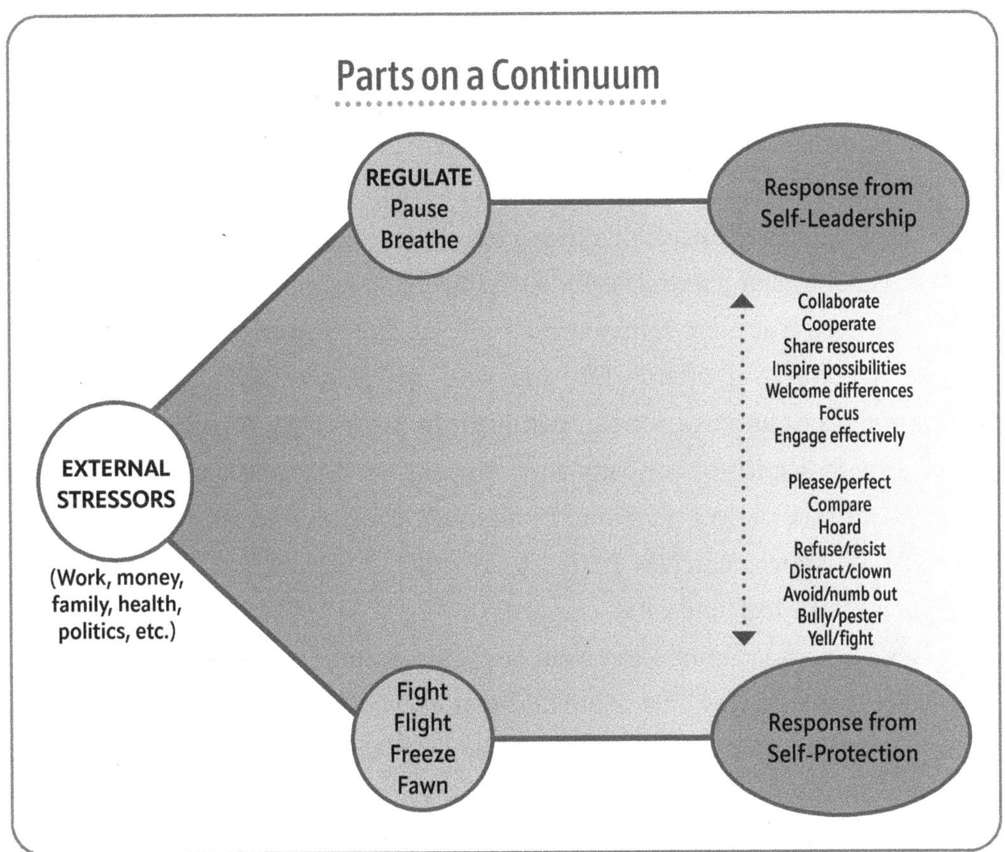

A Leader for Our Parts

On what we might call a good day, our parts operate harmoniously, taking turns at the wheel driving our lives when their role is called upon. Even the students we find most challenging have their good days, right? With that said, intense demands, new lesson content, and social tensions can understandably activate exile parts (feeling inadequate or out of control) which then activates numerous protectors—perhaps a "get organized" part, a "put on your game face" part, a "please everyone" part, and a "defend your honor" part. With numerous protectors on duty at once, we might experience what we call a *parts party*, like a playground full of students with no one on recess duty. When too many of these parts bubble up to the surface, we may even feel flooded or confused. The actions of these parts are not essentially bad or wrong, but with this many voices and personalities together, they work best with leadership, acknowledgment, and direction for how to share the space and get along. In these cases, it can help to take time to name or write down the many different parts or responses that are arising as a way to acknowledge them. This in itself often brings a feeling of relief. We then can follow up by checking with the parts that most need attention right now.

Just as parents or guardians guide a family and teachers run a classroom, our parts also need a leader: someone to facilitate the conversation, acknowledge everyone's voice, and offer a fair and wise perspective. When we step back from the play of our parts, we can rest into the perspective of Self—sitting with ourselves with a spirit of curiosity and compassion. Connected to Self, our own center, we are the perfect person to bring inner leadership to our family of parts. After all, we know ourselves better than anyone, including what we've been through, what we feel, and what we need.

When we approach our parts from Self, they naturally relax and regulate how they express themselves, just as a child settles when a caring adult sits next to them. To relate to our parts, we can deliberately enter our inner dialogue: that conversation always happening in our heads. One by one, we can focus on our parts, acknowledge their intentions, and attend to their needs. In doing this, we offer them the nurturing relationship and genuine connection they may have missed at an earlier point in our lives. While the original experience that caused a part to exist may be over now, the part itself is still very alive and active within us. Through real-time relationship with Self, parts can release outdated beliefs and adopt beneficial roles in our system. When led by Self, our parts can shift from being extreme and protective to manifesting in joyful, effective ways. With practice, and over time, we grow a new and healthy internal environment for our family of parts. They operate as a collaborative team and share their unique skills and perspectives in useful ways for the benefit of the whole. In a nutshell, this is the portal to experience inner peace and true self-care. The following image offers a way to conceptualize this inner team of parts, appreciating that Self is always present, in the center, regardless of how extreme some of the other parts may seem.

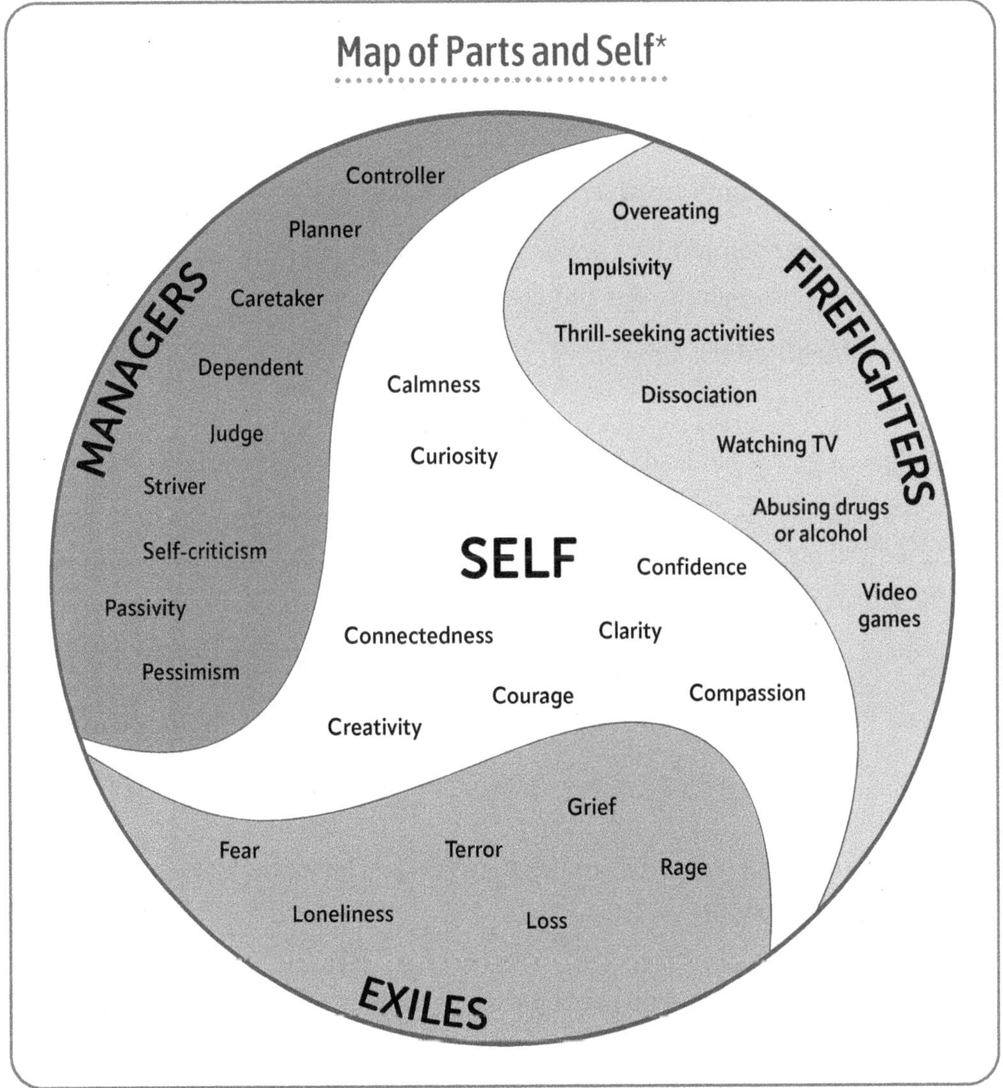

* Adaptation of graphic by Janet R. Mullen, LCSW.

Take a moment to consider what a Self-led team of parts might look like for you. Perhaps there are Self-led parts you already recognize in yourself, parts you would like to nurture and bring forth. Maybe there are additional Self-led parts you would like to work on cultivating in yourself. This list shows examples of skillful parts that would be beneficial for an educator:

- **Receptive listener:** present, attuned, and compassionate to others
- **Effective communicator:** confident and clear as a speaker, teacher, and leader
- **Courageous decision-maker:** able to set boundaries, take risks, and stand for values
- **Collaborative colleague:** able to partner, problem-solve, and innovate with others
- **Playful company:** creative, fun, and friendly
- **Connected companion:** available and loyal to offer mutual support and company through the ups and downs of life
- **Wonder-filled thought partner:** ever-curious, ready to learn, and open to others' ideas

Imagine if you could lead this inner team, allowing these parts to collaborate and choosing which part to act from in any given moment, easefully and deliberately. This is the essence of self-awareness, the heart of self-compassion, and the gift of Self-leadership.

Pause and Reflect

- What if right now you felt calm and connected to yourself? What might be different?
- What if right now you rested into compassion and let it flow into your next interaction with others?
- What if right now your fears and hesitation stepped back and you could move forward, leading with confidence and courage?

Stories from the Field

Learning from the Moment

Kirsten Sanderson is a former international baccalaureate coordinator and curriculum specialist at an elementary school in Connecticut.

After learning about IFS and Self-leadership, I was blown away by the changes I felt in myself. I was able to experience my parts visually and, at times, listen to what they had to say, armed with the "All parts are welcome" mantra. Knowing the 8 Cs and having the sun visual (that shows the sun as a metaphor for Self) really helped me to experience Self while meditating or doing breathwork. Working alongside another teacher at my school, we decided that curiosity was a great go-to strategy when we or someone else was out of Self.

More challenging for me was being able to identify in the moment when I was "flipped" (or *blended*, as IFS refers to inner parts taking over) and then do something about it. I could see in hindsight what I should have done, but I didn't see it in the moment when I was out of Self. The first time I experienced success at this was after a meeting with three colleagues. The meeting did not go as I had hoped, and I felt really frustrated. I felt I was being attacked and responded from a frustrated part. It felt like I was out of sync and unable to connect productively with my colleagues. As the meeting ended, I couldn't join in the friendly small talk. This felt not like me, and I thought they probably noticed this in my body language.

After the meeting, I wondered, *What is wrong with me? Why couldn't I pull myself together?* It occurred to me that by asking these questions, I was being curious, although not compassionate. As I took a few minutes to breathe and reflect, I had the "Aha!" of awareness that I was blended with a part. I realized that the needs-to-be-right part of me was active; with this realization, I unblended and felt better. I remembered my Self-leadership coach guiding me to remember that in Self, I *know* what to do, that I've got this. With this understanding, my part seemed to step back or perhaps lean into my Self. I remembered how much I like and respect my colleagues and sent them a short email thanking them for their time. I also admitted that I didn't feel like my best self at the meeting and asked if we could talk again. Within minutes, all three responded to my email saying that they didn't feel like their best selves either. This experience paved the way for us to work much more effectively the next time we met. I learned how to pause in the moment, respond to feelings like frustration and anxiety by being aware, and, with that awareness, unblend.

These experiences with adults helped me to feel more compassionate when a student was upset or being disruptive. Knowing that they were acting from a part helped me to respond more compassionately. I could find the curiosity I had directed inward and think, *This student seems to feel threatened. I wonder what part of them this is?* Repeating the "All parts are welcome" mantra and using curiosity as my initial response helped me shift my perception of and responses to students. One big benefit of this approach was that it was not a list of things to do or a script, but the essential resources that, with use, can become ingrained in my interactions with myself and others.

The *A* of PAUSE: Being Aware of and Relating to Our Parts

What happens when you pause to be aware of yourself? Perhaps you notice your actions or physical experience, or you tune into your thoughts, feelings, reactions, or needs. Maybe this awareness then allows you to understand yourself a bit better or see your role in what is happening—how you are interacting or impacting the dynamics. Awareness offers a rich portal to access choice and self-empowerment: we can discover how we are being and showing up.

Now let's consider the power and potential of awareness if we apply our understanding that we have a core Self and a team of parts at play. We've learned that we all have parts and these parts take turns rising and subsiding within us as they feel called to respond to our external realities. Within moments, we can flow from our mama bear part to our "do it my way" teenager part to a terrified five-year-old part to our "go get a donut" part. It's rare that we consciously track which part of us is driving the bus, let alone experience that we are the inner team leader. Rather, our day is often experienced as an ebb and flow of various reactions, sensations, and emotions. Swirling in a soup of parts, we sometimes feel we have no power to step into inner leadership—or perhaps free will at all. This brings us to the *A* of the PAUSE model: being *aware* of ourselves.

Being aware, is an invitation to be with ourselves and ask, *Where am I coming from?* Having paused in step one, we now purposefully shift our attention inside and move into relationship with ourselves. We scan to notice thoughts, feelings, and sensations. We learn to differentiate the parts of us that show up; we can see their positive intentions, hear their messages, and recognize how they are trying to help. In this state of awareness, we find space to notice what is operating inside us, who is leading our lives. We can be the observer of our inner team, keeping company with our parts and offering the essential leadership they need to operate as a unified and harmonious team. Yes, all the relational and leadership skills we've cultivated to work with *others* can be turned inside to apply in our relationship with ourselves!

As with pausing, this invitation to turn our attention within and be aware of where we are coming from might feel new. It may feel uncomfortable, or even impossible. In this section, we will cover a very simple and safe process to discover and relate to our parts, one at a time. We will learn how we can build relationships and lead our inner team so we are more centered and ready to lead our lives.

"I remember figuring out why it was called *Self-leadership*. I was confused as to why this term kept being used until it finally clicked for me in an 'Aha!' moment. I remember thinking that we as teachers are leaders, and as leaders, we've got to be able to lead ourselves before we can lead others. We need to be able to recognize our different parts when they show up, understand that they are just parts, and learn not to react from them. This made a lot of sense to me."

—**Carrie Howe,** elementary art teacher

Connecting with Our Parts

Before we get into specific tools for being with our parts, let's recognize the essence of this practice: building connection on the inside. I invite you to picture your parts as little people—little "yous"—all evolved through your experience with the purpose of storing what you've learned about survival so you can get your needs met. Holding them in this way, you may recognize how useful, loyal, and even beloved they are. Truly, there are no bad parts. With this perspective,

I invite you to hold a spirit of curiosity and compassion as you get to know your inner family. What if you didn't need to manage, compartmentalize, control, or judge these different parts? Imagine the amount of energy you would reclaim! What if you could safely and purposefully be with your parts, one at a time, so they could tell you their story, perspective, and underlying longing? After all, who can understand them better than you?

As you are listening to a part, as in any nurturing relationship, a conversation may unfold. Perhaps you will hear a valuable message from your parts or recognize the important role they play. From this, a natural response may arise in you, to acknowledge them, to say, "I get it" or even "Thank you." Just as you would in a loving relationship, you then might wonder what this part of you needs and how you can help. So often, what arises in this work is a simple need to be accepted and appreciated. As parts learn to see us as an adult that is loving and capable, they begin to feel assurance and recognize we can assist them; they don't have to forge on alone. A connection is built. We are in Self-leadership, caring for our parts and poised to lead them as our team. In connecting with our parts, we are building a deep and loving relationship with ourselves, holding the whole of who we are. This is the heart of self-compassion.

Considerations for Awareness Practices

Now that you have a sense of what awareness involves, the next section will delve into specific practices you can integrate into your daily life to relate to parts and lead from Self. For this, always remember that *you* are in charge of your exploration and *you* hold the wisdom about what your system needs. Given this, choose the pace and depth that works for you. At each step in the process, check for signs of Self: Am I still *curious*, do I feel *calm*, can I access *compassion* for myself and these parts? If at any time you lose touch with signs of Self, if you feel flooded or overwhelmed, step back and slow down. With time, the more you invest in knowing your own parts, the more you will be prepared to welcome, understand, and engage with the many parts that show up in others, especially your students.

In the therapeutic realm, IFS provides a thorough road map to know, heal, and build inner harmony among our inner family of parts with the guidance of a trained mental health professional. However, for the sake of our work in schools, the simplified practices in this book can be easily and safely followed by anyone. You don't have to be trained as a therapist or go to a therapist to work with your parts.

If you are interested in learning more about the full IFS healing model or would like to work with a trained IFS coach or therapist, visit the IFS Institute at https://ifs-institute.com.

U-BAC: Building a Relationship with Our Parts

The process of building a relationship with a specific part is captured in the acronym U-BAC™: **U**nblend, **B**efriend, and **A**ttend to **C**onnect with a part. This process guides you to become aware of a specific part and enter into a relationship with it. In moments when a part takes over and you don't feel yourself, you can follow U-BAC to recenter in your Self, and from this space, nurture an inner connection with your part.

You may be thinking, *This sounds ridiculous. How can you actually enter into conversation with the parts in your head?* In response to this, consider that you are already in that inner conversation all the time. The U-BAC process gives you an intentional, effective way to enter into this dialogue and constructively connect with your parts. So for now, see if any skeptical parts of you would be willing to step back for a minute and allow you to simply give the process a chance.

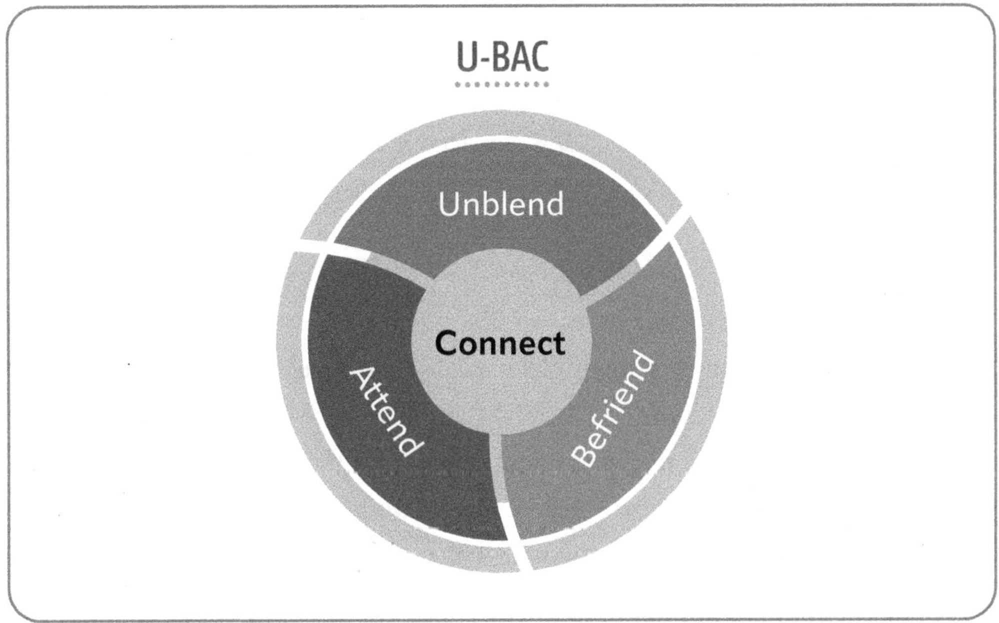

The following table is an overview of the skills in U-BAC that you can follow for building a relationship with a part. We will expand on each in the next sections.

Follow U-BAC

Unblend	*Ask: How do I experience this part right now?* Choose the part you want to focus on, noticing how it shows up through thoughts, feelings, or sensations. Consider this part of you as a distinct inner being and invite it to be with you.
Befriend	*Ask: What is this part's message or motive right now?* From a place of curiosity, ask the part questions that help you understand where it is coming from in this situation and how it is trying to help you.
Attend	*Ask: What does this part of me need right now?* Explore what this part of you needs right now. You can offer the 4 As: acceptance, appreciation, assurance, and assistance.
Connect	Being with your part through the three previous steps allows you to connect with it; in doing so, you are ready to reconnect with the present moment and your capacity in the situation at hand.

Unblend to Connect

When we are *blended* with a part, we may not even realize the part is driving our responses. We just *are* mad, putting on a game face, or obligated to be helpful. In this state, we often aren't aware of the option to choose how we are showing up and engaging. The first step of U-BAC, *unblending*, is a powerful skill that allows us to experience space from our parts and their stories.

TRACKING OUR PARTS

To begin unblending from our parts, we first need to be aware of them and notice their signals by activating our inner observer. We can detect a part by noticing our thoughts, feelings, and sensations. It might also help us to visualize or externalize our parts in some way; we might use a mind map, a figurine, or an image as a way to identify and differentiate from the part. As we practice tracking these inner shifts, we realize these are often signs of our parts and we become familiar with the patterns of our parts as they rise and subside through the course of a day.

This practice of detecting and tracking our parts activates a mindful state in which we see and are free to be with our parts, but we are no longer identified with them. In this way, we can pause and have mini check-ins with our parts throughout the day, and then when we have more time, we can give our full focus on listen in to our team of parts and see who needs attention at that time.

When we unblend from a specific "focus" part, we can invite our part to come into relationship with us, offering that they can separate a little bit and give us a bit of breathing space to be with them. As we differentiate from the reactive thoughts and impulses of the part, we might notice a shift out of fight-or-flight mode into a calmer physiology. This sets us up to keep company with our part in a more Self-led way, with curiosity and compassion. This is the critical starting point for a relationship with any part.

Try this for yourself right now. Pause for a moment and shift your attention inside. Notice your inner experience. Do you pick up on physical cues or sensations? Can you hear what is on your mind? Do you sense a certain feeling inside? Now pick just one of these cues that stands out. What if this is a part that is communicating with you? Now imagine you could see what it looks like, hear it talking to you, or sense why this experience is "on top"—or active in the field of your awareness—for you right now. This is how you start to detect your parts and build a connection with them.

CHOOSE A FOCUS PART

In order to get to know our parts, we focus on one at a time, even if multiple parts of us are reacting and wanting attention (just like when you mediate a group of students who need to take turns to be heard). How then do we determine which part to focus on? The simple answer is to ask inside. Our system knows where we need to focus. In this inner dialogue, remember that *all parts are welcome.* In fact, just like with our students, it is sometimes the most disruptive or persistent part that most needs our attention. Other signals that a part needs attention may be when it surfaces repeatedly as a concern, chatters in the back of our consciousness, dominates our mood, comes out unintentionally in our behavior or relationships, or just won't leave us alone until we pay attention. Parts often repeatedly send us signals, like a brightly colored flag saying, "I am in here. I need you to listen and understand. Pay attention. I have a message for you." Generally, you don't have to look hard to notice what part or parts of you are on top. Finally, you don't need to know what kind of part you are relating to, whether it's a manager, firefighter, or exile. The U-BAC steps apply for all parts, so trust the wisdom of your system.

HOW DO YOU EXPERIENCE YOUR PART RIGHT NOW?

Once we identify a part, we notice how we experience it. Describe (or write down) how you experience the part. Include physical sensations, images, feelings, thoughts, or impulses. This experience will probably correlate with the signs of stress you've previously identified for yourself.

As you work with a part, you might realize it has a name; this helps you identify this aspect of yourself. For example you might say, "My grumpy side," "My indecisive tendency," or "My impulse to just fix it!" Sometimes using these tips to just start to notice our parts is enough to allow our system to subside. We feel the qualities of Self rising up and we are curious to get to know this part. Other times, different parts block a feeling of connection to our focus parts.

HOW DO YOU FEEL TOWARD YOUR PART?

When we choose a part to focus on, we may quickly realize it brings up many mixed feelings. For example, maybe a part of us is angry about a current situation and we decide to make it our "focus part," but other parts of us don't want to indulge anger or are scared that anger could overtake us. If we are going to build a relationship with the angry part, it needs to feel safe with us (just like when we want to authentically connect with another person). Here's what to do: Place your attention on your focus part and internally ask, *How do I feel* toward *this part?* Notice what comes up. You might think:

- "I hate this part. I wish it would go away."
- "This part of me causes so much trouble."
- "If I give it attention, it will just take over."

Maybe there are feelings of criticism, annoyance, or impatience. These are all signs of other parts reacting to the focus part. Generally, if the answer to *How do you feel toward this part?* is not some form of one of the 8 Cs, then there's another part "in the room." Here you can use your Self detector. See if you feel some degree of curiosity, compassion, or connection. Detect if you have a sense of courage, confidence, or clarity being with the part. Notice if there is even a little bit of calm or a sense that there could be creative possibilities.

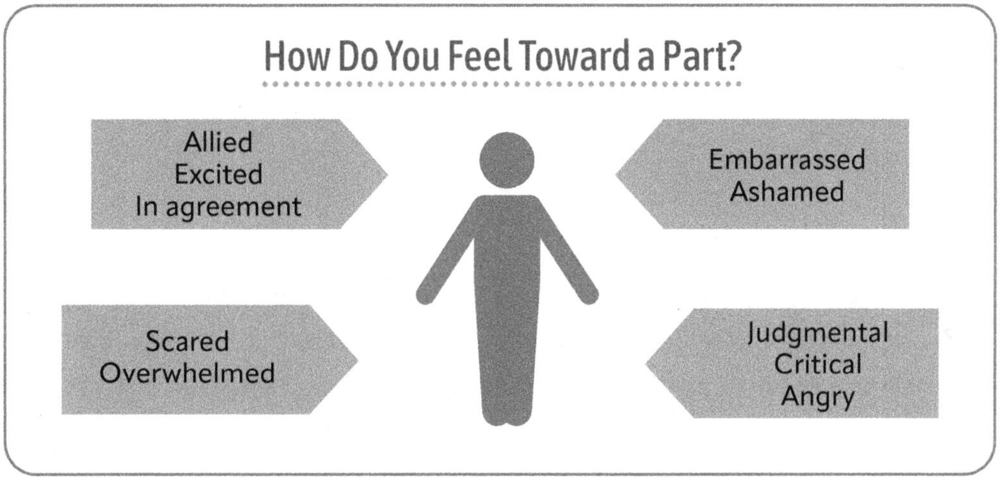

Let's picture this inner process with parts occurring in a conference room or at a kitchen table. To create space to be with your focus part, try asking the reacting parts to step back, much like you do with the unblending process; they can then take a seat in the circle. This is not unlike external relationships when, in a moment of conflict, we need to put down our judgments and agendas and shift into our heart to be with the other person. With practice, we can offer this same spirit of concentrated compassion even to our "problematic" parts—the parts we have spent our lives resisting, even battling; the ones we often call bad habits, irrational, character defects, or unacceptable. Imagine the possibilities if we could learn to relate peacefully with these aspects of ourselves and understand them!

Stories from the Field

The Power of Unblending

Kareen Flores is an elementary educator in California.

Being a teacher comes with many challenges, and each school year presents different obstacles as well. This has been true in all the grade levels I have taught, including my current role as a fourth-grade teacher. One challenge that has remained constant throughout my 10 years of teaching is the feeling of there not being "enough." Not enough time in the day, not enough of me to give each child the attention they deserve, and sometimes not enough energy to give each day 100 percent of me.

Learning to unblend has become my saving grace, as it allows me to create space for and from my parts—the parts that don't want to make mistakes; the parts that are filled with guilt when I am exhausted and can't give my students everything they deserve; the parts that feel that I have failed unless every single one of my students is succeeding at all times; and the parts that want to serve all my students, colleagues, superiors, and students' parents and families. By unblending with these parts, I understand that while they may have beautiful intentions, they can also be so overwhelming that they become a hindrance.

Unblending has taught me that my parts' intentions aren't necessarily bad. It is only a challenge when parts are beating me down or have taken over my system in such a way that I cannot fulfill my intention in my most productive, peaceful, and positive self. By unblending, I can offer attention to those parts of me that get very worked up, and this helps me understand them and work alongside them instead of feeling consumed by them. By pausing to create some space and bring some curiosity and compassion to my parts, I am able to get room to breathe and fulfill my role as a teacher from a place that feels caring—not only for my students, but for myself as well.

Befriend to Connect

The second part of U-BAC, *befriending*, captures the essence of what is needed when we come into relationship with a part. With a new friend, we approach gently and respectfully, putting aside judgment and assumptions. We engage in a conversation to build connection, asking about their interests, their work, and what matters to them. Befriending a part is nearly the same! As we learn to build deeper relationships with our parts, keep in mind that the heart of the process is simply building a loving, safe connection in which our parts trust us, feel understood, and become ready to work for the good of the system.

With Self qualities, especially curiosity, we can ask questions to understand our part's message and motive. Questions to ask our part include:

- What is your message for me right now?
  - What do you want me to know?
  - What is your story or perspective? Where are you coming from?
  - What is important to you? Why?

You can also ask questions to tune in to a part's positive intent:

- What is your motive or mission right now?
  - How are you trying to help me? What is your role?
  - How are you trying to protect me? What are your fears or concerns?

As you experiment asking these questions, your own intuition may take over at some point, guiding you as to what question to ask or what gesture of compassion your part needs. Again, it is all about building connection. Trust yourself and go for it!

Attend to Connect

When we befriend a part, we discover where it is coming from and how it is trying to help us. Following this, the third step of U-BAC is when we *attend* to the part's underlying or core needs in this moment or situation. How do we know what these are? We ask the part—it will tell us. Instead of allowing your smart, problem-solving fixer or caregiver parts to step in and figure out what needs to happen, picture yourself asking the part, *What do you need right now?* and then listening to its needs.

We can often find what our parts need by using the 4 As: acceptance, appreciation, assurance, and assistance. While not comprehensive, our needs often boil down to one of these common needs:

1. **Acceptance:** Parts want to feel welcomed as they are, accepted for their uniqueness and differences, and included regardless of perceived mistakes. Speaking to a part of yourself you might say, "I accept you just as you are. You are welcome to be here with me."
2. **Appreciation:** Parts often work very hard for us. It is powerful to thank them for their role and effort. They feel valued for their positive intent, even if the actual impact wasn't ideal. Speaking to a part of yourself, you might say, "Thank you for all you do, trying to help and protect me. I see how hard you work and appreciate your positive intent."
3. **Assurance:** Parts frequently feel isolated and alone, frozen in our past. They may need comfort from us through words or affection. Also, it can be reassuring for them to be updated on your actual level of safety and capability as an adult. Speaking to a part of yourself, you might offer, "You are not alone. I am here, an adult, and I am smart, loving, and capable. We are okay right now."
4. **Assistance:** A part may need us to take specific concrete action or make changes. Sometimes our part needs us to stand in our power and speak *for* it out loud to others. As parts formed at times when we were less resourceful and capable, we can update them with the recognition of who we are now: an adult who survived (and even thrived!) and can figure this out too! Speaking to a part of yourself, you might say, "I am here to help. I've faced many challenges, and I can figure it out one step at a time. I also have many resources around me that I can call on as needed."

As we attune and respond to our parts' needs, they feel our presence, support, and leadership. Rather than being subject to an overwhelmed, overburdened young part, our system can start to experience our true maturity and capacity as an adult. Physically and psychologically, we shift from a self-protective stress state in which we perceive life as a threat into a confident, regulated, integrated state from which we can powerfully take the reins and lead our lives.

Connect

By taking time to unblend, befriend, and attend, we *connect* with our part. Through this process of connection, we help them feel understood, supported, and not alone. Updated on who we are and what we are capable of, parts soften and allow space for us to step forward in a more mature, Self-led way. We are then ready to proceed with connecting with others and the situation before us. We can choose how we wish to engage, perhaps purposefully calling up one of the 8 C qualities or identifying a more Self-led or mature part of us to take the lead. In this sense, connection is not a distinct step, but what we are cultivating through the previous three steps.

The following image depicts what building a relationship looks like with our different kinds of parts when we use U-BAC. Through this practice, we rest into Self to keep company with our parts.

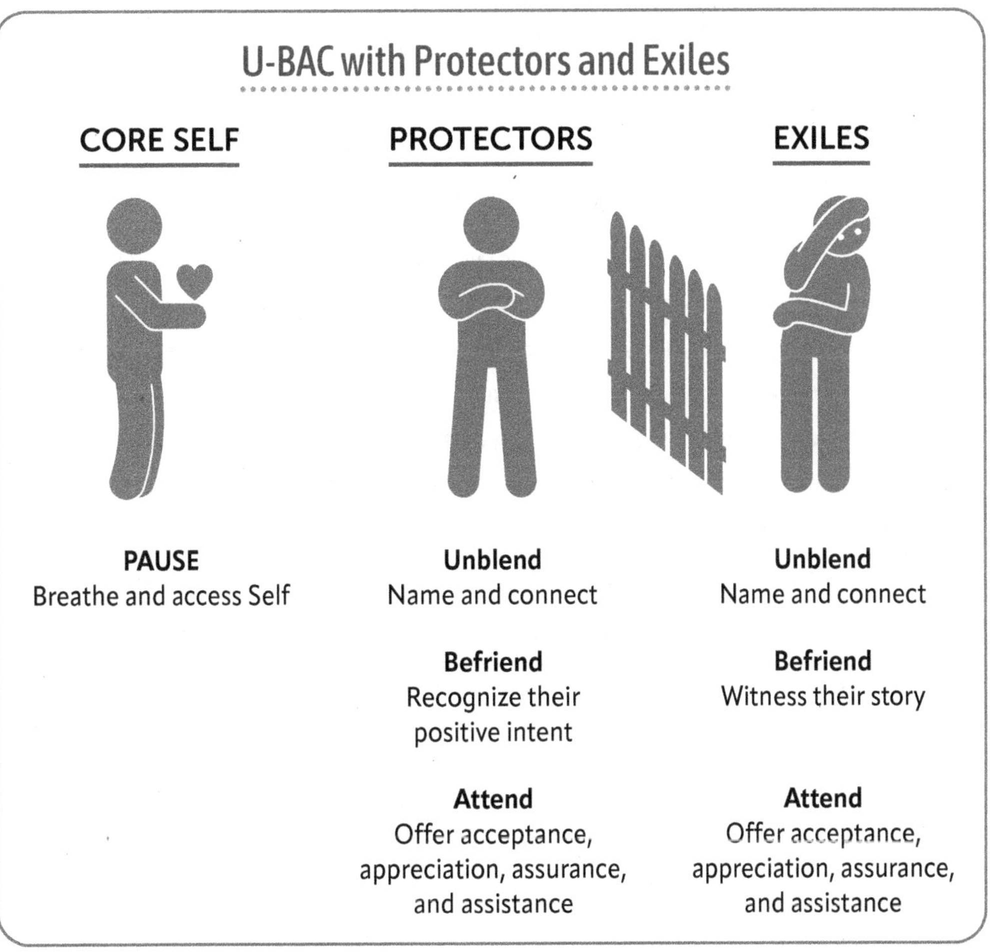

Conclusion

Many of us tend to spend our days functioning primarily from protective parts: trying to teach, control, get cooperation, or be the expert. The result may be that we feel overwhelmed, burned out, inadequate, and exhausted. It's not sustainable. By contrast, when we practice moving through our day connected to more Self-led parts, we find our time to be much more inspiring, hopeful, collaborative, and even rejuvenating.

Educators and parents alike report what a relief it is to realize this new way of operating. While we never reach a state where we practice perfect Self-leadership all the time—it is always a dynamic practice—we can hold awareness of Self, be kind to ourselves as we attend to our parts, and gradually increase the moments when we embody Self-leadership.

Stories from the Field

Following U-BAC to Befriend Parts

Pavlina Gatikova is an English as a second language teacher for a public school district in Massachusetts.

It's August 2021, and as the new school year is about to begin, I notice a lot of parts vying for my attention. One that announces itself most strongly is very concerned about my ability to begin the year in a "perfect" manner. I will call this my Perfect Pav part. She informs me that I have not done any preparation so far, haven't tried to read up on anything that would be connected to my teaching, and haven't even set up my classroom. I have just been relaxing and enjoying myself in non-work-related ways. Perfect Pav has even more to say, but you've got the idea. I decide that I want to better understand this part, so I set aside time to follow the U-BAC process.

Unblending: As I scan inside, I notice this Perfect Pav part resides in my throat; I can sense constriction there as I focus on the part. It feels as if someone's holding me and putting pressure on my neck, like a hose that someone is squeezing with their hands in order to stop the flow of water. This part is very close to me, and I ask her to give me a little breathing space. I ask myself, *How do I feel toward this part?* In this moment, another part of me wants Perfect

Pav to go away; it feels she is intimidating and too big for me to handle. I notice that these feelings are coming from a younger part of me. I reassure her and ask her to step back. She does.

I check again and ask, *How do I feel toward the Perfect Pav part now?* Ah . . . I am feeling more curiosity and compassion for Perfect Pav—I am ready to connect with her. I ask Perfect Pav what she can tell me about herself and how she's trying to help me.

Befriending: As I sit inwardly with this part, I get a clear sense that I am with a young part of myself. I sense she is scared but also can be very strong. Quite simply, her job is to protect me by making sure I do things so other people will love, welcome, and accept me—and never ignore, reject, or abandon me. She wants me to know how helpful she is, and that she steps in to make sure I won't make any mistakes. A shift happens inside me. I feel the positive intent of this part, working so hard to make sure others will love me.

Out of curiosity I ask, *If you didn't have to do your job the way you are doing it now, what would you rather do?*

Perfect Pav quickly replies, "I'd swing in a hammock and listen to the birds chirping above and have an adult sing me some beautiful songs. I could even take a nap, which I would much rather do."

So then I ask, *What do you think would happen if you didn't do your job?*

Perfect Pav replies, "I am afraid you would no longer work your hardest and you'd lose people you love and your job. Then your life would be miserable, unhappy, and lonesome."

I respond, *Thank you, Perfect Pav, for sharing with me. This has been really helpful and it all makes sense now. Your effort has been more than heroic, and I really appreciate that.*

Attending: I then sense that this part needs assurance that I am here and that I am a capable adult, so I say, *I would like to reassure you that from now on, I (adult Pavlina) can assist you and can even take the bulk of the work off your shoulders. How does that sound?*

Perfect Pav says, "That sounds perfect!"

Connecting: Following this inner dialogue, I can feel a shift inside as I imagine preparing for teaching and returning to school. Sure, there is still a lot to do, many expectations, and the possibility of imperfections. The difference is in where I am coming from. Rather than feeling overwhelmed and self-critical, I am able to access a place of calm and confidence, remembering that I am a competent and dedicated teacher. While I can't anticipate and perfectly plan for every eventuality, I can show up connected to my Self, offer my focus and compassion, and trust that I'm more than good enough. This is such a tangible and profound shift for me in my perception and experience of the start of school. What a gift!

Invitations to Practice

REFLECT: *Unblending for Breathing Space*

Find a comfortable posture in which your breath can easily flow. Shift your attention to your inner space, resting your attention on your breath. Scan inside, noticing what parts of you are present right now. They may show up as thoughts, feelings, sensations, images, or the voices in your inner conversation. As you notice each, acknowledge it and then, with your next exhale, invite that part to separate a little bit. Picture that part floating out on your breath like a balloon. It can then hang in the air around you, connected by a string. You are not getting rid of your parts; they are not floating away. Rather, you are creating breathing space to be *with* them. Continue noticing your parts and exhaling them as balloons. Notice as you start to experience the qualities of Self. As you start to feel a bit of calm or curiosity, breathe out these qualities as a gift to your parts. Invite them to connect with you. Following this reflection, record the parts you noticed by writing a list or using the parts map provided on the next page.

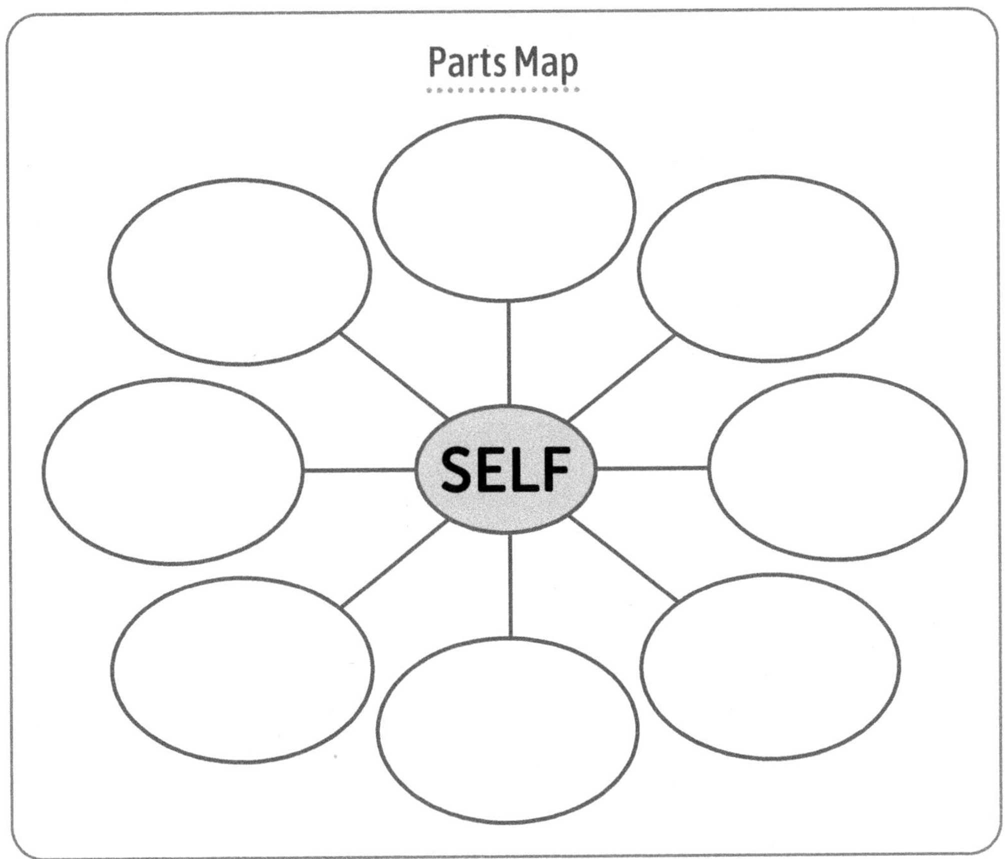

Act: Notice Parts in Daily Life

- Try to notice different parts at play, including how they show up for and in you and others.
- Try unblending on the fly. In a stressful moment, notice what parts are showing up and ask them to step back. Breathe. Access a little more Self. Remember the 8 Cs: calm, compassionate, courageous, curious, confident, clear, creative, and connected.
- Create a map or list of the parts that you've noticed throughout the day.
- Experiment with weaving parts language into your everyday speech.

WALK: *Unblending on the Path*

Take your parts on a walk. As you walk, notice what you are experiencing inside. Whether it's a feeling, thought, physical sensation, or image, consider it a part of you presenting in your consciousness. Acknowledge it. Then ask it to separate. This part can walk with you at your side. It may even be "put down" on the side of the road for you to "pick up" on your return. See what happens if you unblend from your parts so it is just you, out on a walk.

EXPLORE: *Connect with a Focus Part Using U-BAC*

Name the Part: ______________________________

Unblend: How do you experience the part right now? Does it show up in thoughts, feelings, sensations? Be curious.

____

____

____

Befriend: What is this part's message? How is it trying to help right now?

____

____

____

Attend: What does the part need right now? Would it like acceptance, appreciation, assistance, assurance?

____

____

____

Connect: Now that you are connected with your part and preparing to reconnect with others and the situation, decide from what place in yourself you choose to lead. Consider if there is an 8 C quality you want to embody or a more mature or Self-led part ready to act.

____

____

____

CHAPTER 3

Understand Each Other: Nurturing Self-Led Relationships

Pause and Reflect

- Bring to mind a positive moment with a favorite teacher or a significant adult in your childhood. What happened for you in the space of this interaction?
  - How did you feel about yourself?
  - What did they model about how to relate and respond?
- Note what you learned through this relationship. Does it even inform who you are today?

As we learn about the importance of parts and the possibility to lead from Self, we likely wonder how this can benefit students and our everyday relationships with them. Each day we witness students too anxious to come to school, unable to control their emotions, acting as bullies, or struggling with low self-esteem. Over and again, we reach into our toolbox to help. While we know we make a difference, too often we may feel our efforts are insufficient or ineffective. We still see many children falling through the cracks. How can we help?

The understanding of Self and the parts provides a powerful lens through which to glimpse what is happening inside our students and to guide them toward emotional relief, effective communication, and productive engagement in school. Through our everyday interactions, we have the power to unblend from *our* parts and to listen deeply to hold compassion for *theirs*. Along with our students, in more Self-led parts, we will develop more secure, attached, and generative relationships that are foundational for a successful learning experience. When we as educators step into our power, we directly impact our students' sense of Self, their confidence to engage, and even the trajectory of their lives. Chapter 3 will explore the significance of healthy relationships between all members of our school communities and discuss how to cultivate Self-led relationships in the school setting.

In this chapter, we will:

- Explore how the dynamic of our interactions with children contributes to the formation of their parts
- Appreciate how to show up with greater Self-leadership by listening and speaking from Self
- Reflect on how the U-BAC framework brings compassion in daily relationships with others

Development of Parts in Relationships

Life at school is a constant interplay of significant interactions. Students not only learn from their direct interactions with adults, but they also witness how adults relate to students, other adults, and in one-on-one and group contexts. In the container of these relationships, children can cultivate Self-led parts—even students who have experienced hurt and devaluing relationships elsewhere can repair and heal, one corrective interaction at a time. Repeated experiences in relationships develop internal patterns that inform our parts, our sense of Self, and our blueprint for relationships. This is where we practice how to be human. How amazing that as educators we play such an impactful role in this powerful process! Indeed, Self-led relationships rest at the heart of healthy school culture and climate and are a fundamental means to nurture a generation with the capacity to thrive together.

In order to understand how to optimally relate to our students, we will explore how their parts develop in the context of their relationships with primary attachment figures, in this case, us as educators. Most students walk side-by-side with adults every step of the way as they learn to face stressors, navigate choices, and discover their options for response. Take a moment to appreciate the wide array of complex stressors, demands, and messages students face at home and school each day—the stressors we guide them through:

- Homework, tests, new academic content
- Teasing, bullying, peer pressure, exclusion
- Fashion, sexuality, drugs, commercialism
- Family dynamics, expectations, conflict
- World politics, wars, pandemics, climate change

So how do young people learn how to make sense of it all and choose a responsible, beneficial response to a situation? They rely on us to model and coach them. This has been demonstrated in research of secure relational attachments between young children and their caregivers. When an infant's caregiver is not attuned to their needs, the infant forms an insecure attachment system, which limits their ability to cope with stress (Schore, 2000). In other words, when we guide them from a Self-led place, they will be more capable at leading from Self in the future.

The RISE Model

Let's imagine we could put an interaction with a student in slow motion and isolate how we are influencing the development of their parts in a given situation. The acronym RISE can help us depict the elements of interaction between adults and students. (RISE is just intended to illustrate the relational dynamic. PAUSE and U-BAC are the two key acronyms to integrate into our daily practice.) We respond to an external stressor in four stages: *regulate* physically, *integrate* and make meaning, *strategize* our response, and *express* through our behavior. The following image shows this model; we will find out in the next sections that *how* we move toward our expressed behavior depends on if we are leading from Self (the *high road*) or from a more self-protective part (the *low road.*)

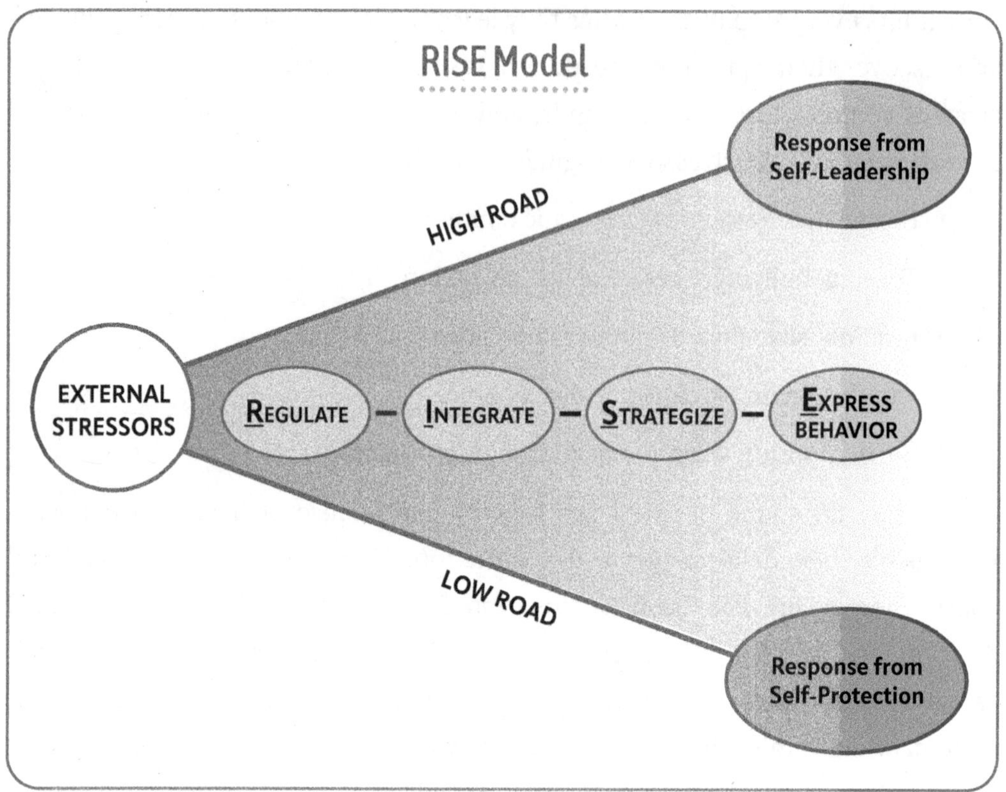

As we reflect further on the elements of RISE, consider how this applies to children's interactions with primary caregivers, parents, and educators, and how all these interactions collectively influence the parts that *RISE* up in our students.

ELEMENTS OF SELF-LED INTERACTIONS (THE HIGH ROAD)

When an adult interacts with a child, the optimal response to an external stressor would be leading from Self. Let's consider how this might look using RISE:

- **Regulate:** In a stressful moment, the adult pauses to check for a reaction in themselves. They breathe and regulate their own nervous system. As they stay in or shift back into a calm physiology, this sends a nonverbal signal to the child's nervous system. The adult may also coach the child to regulate physically or validate how they are feeling: "Let's pause and just take a breath. I know that was a little scary. We're okay." Through these gestures, the adult communicates, *I am here.*

- **Integrate:** Next, the adult helps the child interpret and figure out what is happening. Ideally, the adult acknowledges what is happening outside while reinforcing that both the adult and the child have the capacity to respond effectively—to cope. The child integrates a story about the situation and corresponding beliefs about themselves: "Something bad may be happening *outside* me, but *I* am not bad; we are together and we can handle this."
- **Strategize to thrive:** Following this, an adult takes responsibility and considers what needs to be done. They reflect on different options, assess resources, and consider implications of their actions for all involved. The child watches and may be involved in the process or discussion about how to problem-solve and prepare for a skillful response.
- **Express Self-led behavior:** Finally, the adult takes action in whatever way is needed. Again, the child may be learning by watching or they may be engaged in action, walking side-by-side with the adult. In this process they see how it's done, experiencing their own agency to choose and power to do something in response to the difficulty.

As a result of repeated experiences like this, the child learns how to be a calm, connected, and effective human being. The child develops self-awareness, knowledge, and skills to navigate life challenges successfully. The child practices engaging their body, mind, and heart in regulated, integrated action, and this practiced response cultivates Self-led parts. Even by the time this child shows up for kindergarten, they will have a toolbox of Self-led parts to draw on so they can be confident taking a risk, helping a friend, cooperating in a group, and persisting when something doesn't work. Through the ongoing modeling of their caregivers and educators, this child will develop an innate sense of their worth and capacity, as well as the courage to reach out and collaborate with others. An underlying foundation of resilience is built into their system, and when more difficult circumstances present, their parts are prepared to make meaning of it, stay connected with others, and work toward productive action.

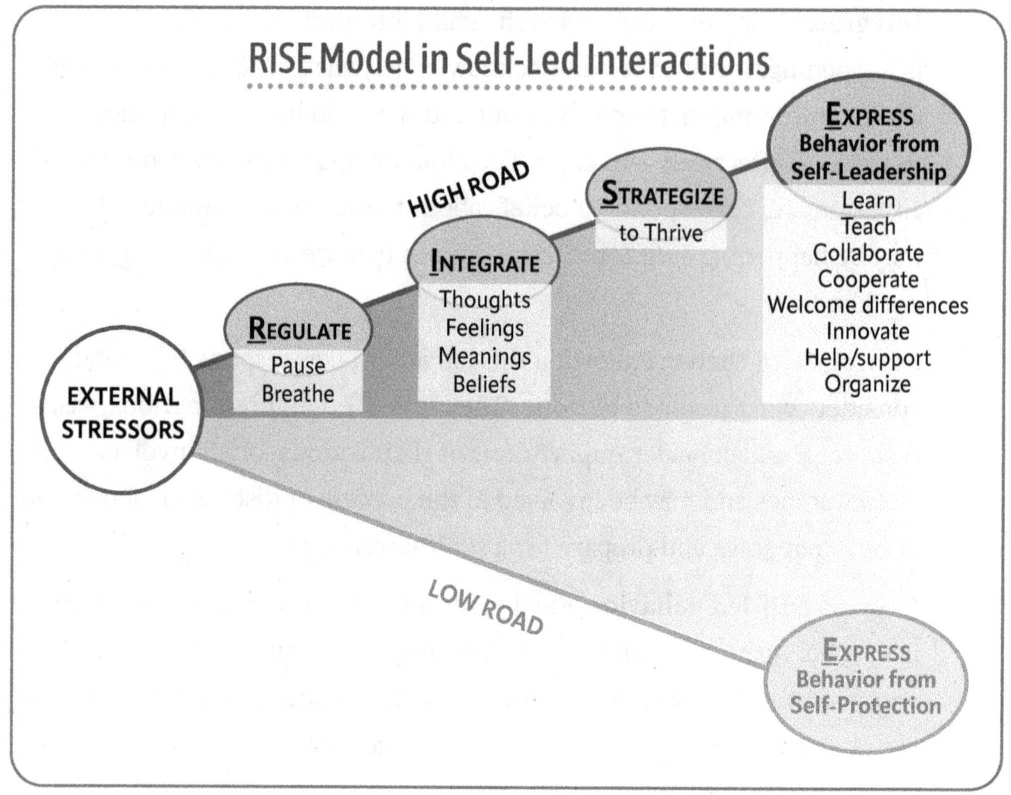

ELEMENTS OF SELF-PROTECTIVE INTERACTIONS (THE LOW ROAD)

Now let's consider when an adult's response is less Self-led. This could happen even when the most well-intentioned and relatively skillful parents and educators are distracted, overwhelmed, or having a hard day. This could also take place when an adult is suffering from their own losses or living with unhealed trauma. What happens then?

- **Dysregulate (fight, flight, freeze, fawn):** If an adult perceives a stressor as something dangerous that they cannot handle, they will go into a stress response to some degree in their own body (i.e., fight, flight, freeze, or fawn). This can present in many ways. For example, they may experience a physical shift feeling more anxious and irritable. There will also likely be a corresponding shift in behavior such as becoming withdrawn, unpredictable or even aggressive. From the adult's behavior in response to the stressor, the child detects the message, *There is danger. We are not safe.*

Even if words are not spoken, the child's nervous system will respond with an instinctive survival stress response of their own.

- **Dis-integrate:** A reactive physical state compromises the brain functioning of both children and adults. They look at the situation through protective parts that have a more limited, survival-based perspective. As the adult makes sense of the situation and communicates this to the child, they are likely to convey some version of a message like *Bad things are happening*, *We can't handle this*, or *There is something wrong with us*. In this context, a child may internalize blame or feel shame—as if they are inadequate or not good enough. Young people especially are highly identified with their caregivers and won't question the validity of the adult's message, even if the adult is seeing the situation through an extreme part of their own.
- **Strategize to survive:** Feeling vulnerability and shame, the adult will revert to a survival strategy. It is likely they won't perceive options and will automatically resort to protective (often extreme or disproportional) responses to the circumstance. Either explicitly or implicitly, they teach the child that this is the best response to this situation. The adult is teaching what they know, even if it is not relevant to the time and current reality.
- **Express self-protective behavior:** Through repeated experience with adults who are operating from this state of dysregulation and lacking holistic integration, children develop their own automatic survival response strategies. In other words, this is how they develop protective parts.

Protective parts become a child's go-to strategy for ensuring inclusion in their family and community. The more difficult or traumatic a child's experiences, the more extreme and protective their parts may become. These patterns of coping are often passed through generations, whether as minor traits, learned behaviors, or primary mindsets for functioning. Some familiar intergenerational parts include being hypervigilant, needing to be perfect, bullying others to maintain dominance, or thinking one's race, class, or gender is better than another. While these protective parts manifest in many ways, they are established and passed through generations because they are perceived as necessary for survival. (Notice again that our protective parts have a positive intent.) Family patterns of seemingly extreme emotional and behavioral responses are often manifestations of protective parts resulting from intergenerational trauma. Awareness of how parts develop in relationship as explained by the RISE model gives us the keys to see and start the healing process for these parts, one wise and compassionate interaction at a time.

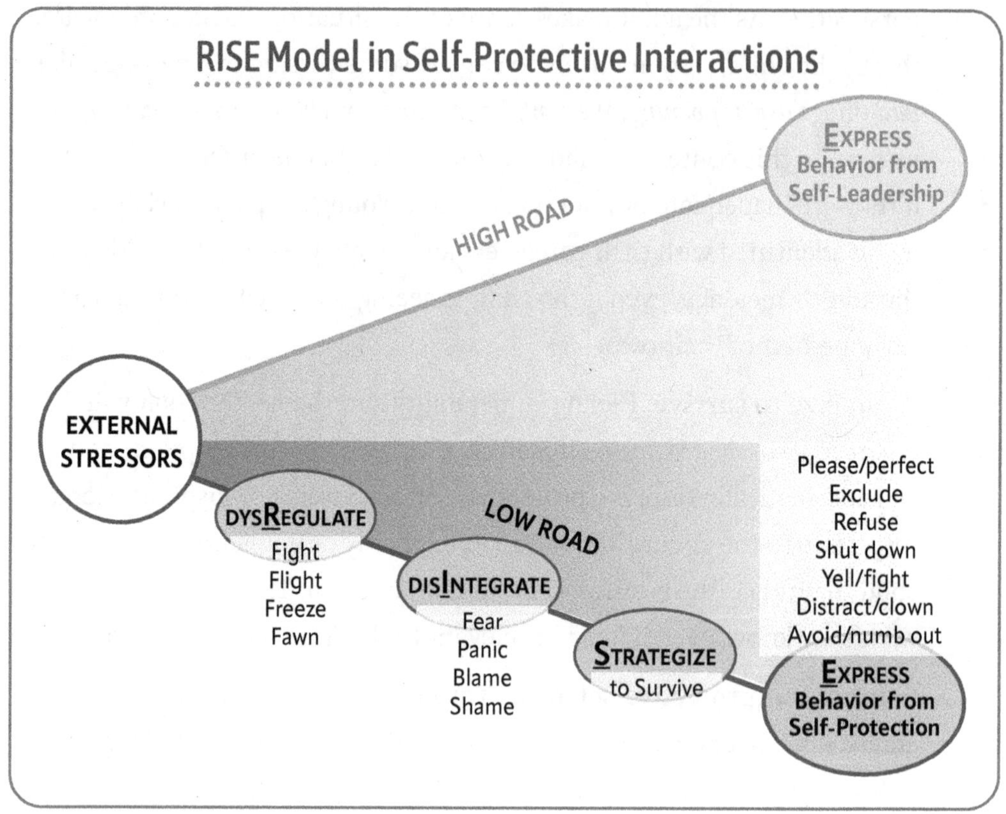

SIGNIFICANCE OF RISE IN SCHOOL

Young people's parts reflect the composite of what they have learned from acute and repeated experience in their family, school, community, and culture. Then in future situations, these are the parts that *rise* up in our students, with protective parts being quite active in schools. We may see the anxious, overachieving student; the quiet, hesitant child; the class clown; the bully on the playground; or the student who refuses to follow directions. These protector parts manifest in students by running interference "on top" to keep exile parts out of sight; therefore, the protectors are especially what we glimpse in our students who have experienced trauma, loss, conflict, and neglect. In comparison to the place and time, these parts may sometimes seem out-of-place, disproportional, disruptive, or noncompliant, but as we know, they believe they are operating as loyal servants committed to the child's preservation and survival. When we start to recognize the origin and purpose underlying our students' parts, it introduces a game-changing paradigm for how we see and respond to their behaviors and underlying needs.

"I have started to do brief reflections with teachers and parents on situations in their lives where basic psychological needs were not fulfilled. I ask them about how it felt in their body, what thoughts, images, and emotions come up, and how they would love to react if they could relive these moments. Then I have them imagine the opposite situation—where every need was fulfilled—and ask them to again feel their body, thoughts, feelings, and images. Finally, I debrief the experiences.

This exercise gives them deep insight into what it feels like when psychological basic needs are not fulfilled and how that burdens our parts and creates protectors. Most important, the adults see their responsibility for children and how they can cause burdens in children with their behavior. After that, we reflect on how they can support children in their psychological needs at school, kindergarten, or home."

—Ann-Katrin Bockman, PhD, psychologist and professor, University of Hildesheim, Germany

---

School-Based Relationship: What Transpires Between Us

We may wonder how educators can have an impact on students' lives when the influences of family life, traumatic experiences, and society are all so significant. While this is understandable, we can also appreciate that each day, as students relate to us, their parts are also present, operating, responding, and alive. This means that parts can continue to learn and evolve. For educators, this offers hope. While therapy and coaching may come into play "downstream"—once a part of a student is established in a problematic pattern—educators are present "upstream," or during the development of parts. As educators, not only can we have compassion for the origin of our students' parts, but we can play a fundamental role in proactively nurturing more Self-led parts. As we model how to relate from Self-leadership, students see and therefore believe that another way of being is possible. We can proactively nurture healthy parts in students and even shift the evolution of more extreme parts. As we simply and gently coach students through daily transitions, difficulties, and interactions, they learn how to relate to themselves and others with compassion. Ultimately, we can guide them to develop the inner compass to navigate life from Self-leadership on their own. In this way, even if they are carrying the scars of trauma, the nature of our daily company is not only comforting and formative but, in fact, healing.

Stories from the Field

The Possibility of Upstream

Tim Amaral is an award-winning teacher from California.

I teach adults who are studying to get their high school equivalency diploma. Each day, I see the downstream effects of upstream trauma and neglect in the lives of my students. As children, my students were often struggling with learning disabilities, mental health challenges, and family trauma, yet many of their teachers saw only pathology: disruptiveness, a lack of motivation, or a challenging behavior. It's my experience that most of the in-school events that escalated into conflict and eventually derailed my students' academic lives were actually quite brief—they lasted from 15 minutes or so to less than 1 minute at times. What if those moments could have been creatively avoided, compassionately redirected, or calmly resolved? What if, instead of classroom disciplinarians, my students had Self-led teachers who were sensitive and responsive adults, able to listen to and meet their needs? To me, having an educator who is trained in Self-leadership be present at an earlier stage in the lives of my students would be invaluable. That person has the potential to redirect the flow of my students' lives—so much so that they might never even become my students.

What Works, What Doesn't, and Why?

Educators already have many wonderful and effective tools that support students to access and act from Self-leadership, though we might not call them that yet. Here are some common practices many educators already use to coach and encourage students:

- Teaching simple self-regulation skills, such as pausing and taking a mindful breath
- Providing inspiring affirmations
- Modeling and encouraging a positive mindset
- Rewarding prosocial, constructive behavior
- Redirecting focus and supporting behavior modification
- Coaching a missing skill set that will position the student for success

Many times, these tools work to assist students in shifting into greater Self-leadership. But when they work, why do they work? Explored through the lens of Self-leadership, we can appreciate that students respond when they can feel that *we* are in Self: calm, compassionate, confident, and clear. When we are in Self, we recognize that the student has numerous sides to them, and we remember and call forth the core goodness and full potential we believe in (the student's Self). And though it may sound simple, when our strategies come from a space of Self-leadership in us and elicit Self-leadership in the student, the strategy works.

"As a longtime educator, when I look back at times when I've felt very successful in coaching social skills and emotional resilience in students, I can identify how I was, in fact, applying the underlying principles of the Self-leadership approach contained in the PAUSE model."

—**Kirsten Sanderson,** retired elementary teacher and curriculum specialist, Connecticut

---

What about when we've tried everything in our toolbox and nothing seems to work? This can be so bewildering! One factor to consider is where the student is at—that is, what part of them is activated, and consequently, how are they hearing and interpreting our direction? Another equally essential key is where we ourselves are *actually* coming from; we need to honestly check if we are Self-led or agenda-driven by parts. Finally, we need to consider the dynamic at play between us, the interconnected system of adult and student.

A common cycle of interaction with students is activated when we focus on a student's external disruptive behavior. We try to figure out where *they* are stuck and how to help them. Our response revolves around getting students to get back on the high road, to make "good choices," and be "compliant and productive." We believe if we give them clear expectations, tools, and encouragement, then they should be able to choose a successful action. Therefore, when a student is not able to shift into the preferred behavior and they stay on the low road, it's not uncommon that many parts of educators are activated—parts that try harder, judge, and control.

Our parts often have a story about this student. Have you ever heard a teacher say to a student, "It's easy. You can do this. You just need to try harder" or "What is wrong with you? Why can't you just follow directions?" They might even comment to a colleague about the student, describing them as difficult, resistant, or manipulative: "He would behave differently if he wanted to. But he's not even trying." "I guarantee you this behavior is on purpose. She knows exactly what she's doing." In comments like this, we can hear a number of parts in us holding assumptions about the student. We believe the student is choosing their behavior and responding to the present situation (versus acting from past experiences or realities outside school). Assuming the student's behavior is on purpose, we often miss what is going on for them and the underlying need of their parts. We miss the opportunity to provide a corrective experience and nurture authentic, Self-led engagement.

In discussing this, some educators might argue that their techniques and strategies do work. For example, when students get called out in front of peers or receive in-school suspension, the teachers and school administrators may say they get results. Perhaps a student gets quieter, stops acting out, and tries harder. While this may be the case, we need to carefully consider what students are *actually* learning in these interactions. Have they grown an increased sense of confidence, courage, and self-compassion, *or* do they have even more shame and pain that will lead them to strategize further how to protect themselves? Is the root of their behavior addressed, *or* will it just surface later in a different and perhaps more extreme way? In the end, the explicit or implicit message a student may take away could be any of the following:

- "There is something wrong with me if I can't do this like everyone else."
- "If I behave this way, I am bad."
- "Adults can't handle and don't accept my difficult emotions."
- "Don't let anyone see what is really going on inside."
- "I have to figure out how to cope on my own."
- "I am stupid."

We can imagine that if a student internalizes these beliefs, they internalize shame, which in turn energizes the need to self-protect. It helps to remember that no one, students included, actually enjoys acting from extreme, reactive, or disruptive parts. Students simply don't see an option to respond differently when they are locked in protective parts. These parts resort to their go-to strategy and escalate communication, waving their brightly colored flag for help until someone responds. All the while, the student still possesses the capacity to be Self-led. If we can put them at ease so Self can emerge, they will intuitively move toward a healthier and more harmonious way of functioning.

How do we do this? Clearly it doesn't work to get into a battle to try to overpower students' parts, fix them, or tell them what to do. We can't stand on the high road and just tell a student to leave the low road. We will only find ourselves exhausted and at odds with the student. Rather, our job is to tether ourselves in Self and then walk side-by-side with the student, who is stuck on the low road, to keep them company. We approach them with curiosity to understand what part is driving them. As their part feels appreciated, it will soften and deescalate, and the student will settle back into a more Self-led way of being.

In my work with students, they have often shared, "I just wish someone would stop and hear my side of the story and get my perspective. I don't need to be right; I just wish they would understand." When we offer space for compassionate communication and are present to students in their experience, acting free of judgment and agenda, they often shift into their inner wisdom and find their own path back to the high road, not only remedying the present situation but building confidence for the future.

Stories from the Field

Taking a Pause and Shifting with Students

Sarah Cerbarano is a fourth-grade teacher in Connecticut.

Based on some of my Self-leadership training, I decided to adjust and experiment a little bit with how I was interacting with my students. What surprised me the most was how quickly the impact happened. There was one student in particular that floored me in terms of how she responded to this slight shift in communication. Rather than reactively asking her questions like "Why didn't you complete this?" or "Why did you choose to _____?" I changed the language: "I am noticing _____ right now. What do you need?" I expected my student to stand there quietly and not respond. However, without hesitation, she said exactly what she needed, which was historically a challenge for her. I could feel the energy between the two of us completely shift in a positive way. From that point, there was no turning back. I learned at that moment the power of this framework. It taught me it was okay to stop and take a pause, and I realized how I could more appropriately evaluate a situation and truly think about what my students and I need to check in with Self. This inner acknowledgment gave me permission to build the PAUSE method into my teaching—to be less reactive and more mindful and proactive in my practices with students and myself. I started to consistently pull students aside and say, "Hey, I am noticing _____. What is up? What do you need? How can I help?" If I was met with resistance or no response, I always let them know that "I am here if you need me or I can reach out to someone else that can be of help." There was no pressure, no judgment. As an educator, the shift and depth of this mindset does not always come so easily. I have learned I will have slip-ups and moments that may not follow this framework. Therefore, I've found it's an ever-evolving practice, one that I am convinced is crucial to building and strengthening the relationships I create with my students each and every school year.

The Interaction of Parts Between Us

Coaching students to develop Self-led parts and Self-led action happens through the nuance of each interaction. To discover how we can enter this dynamic, let's examine how our parts interact in the space of a school day. When two people engage with one another, their parts do as well. This interaction has the potential to flow like an infinity loop, with one person's parts activating the other's. As you can see in the following image, an external stressor has activated the student's vulnerable exile. This causes their protectors to jump into action to protect the student from feeling the underlying pain of the exiled part. In turn, the student's protective behavior impacts the educator's inner experience, touching off the educator's exiles. In response to this, the educator's protectors reveal themselves, rising up to suppress the exile and respond to the student. The educator's protective behavior then cycles back to further touch off parts in the student. In this way, there is a continuous loop of interaction between our parts.

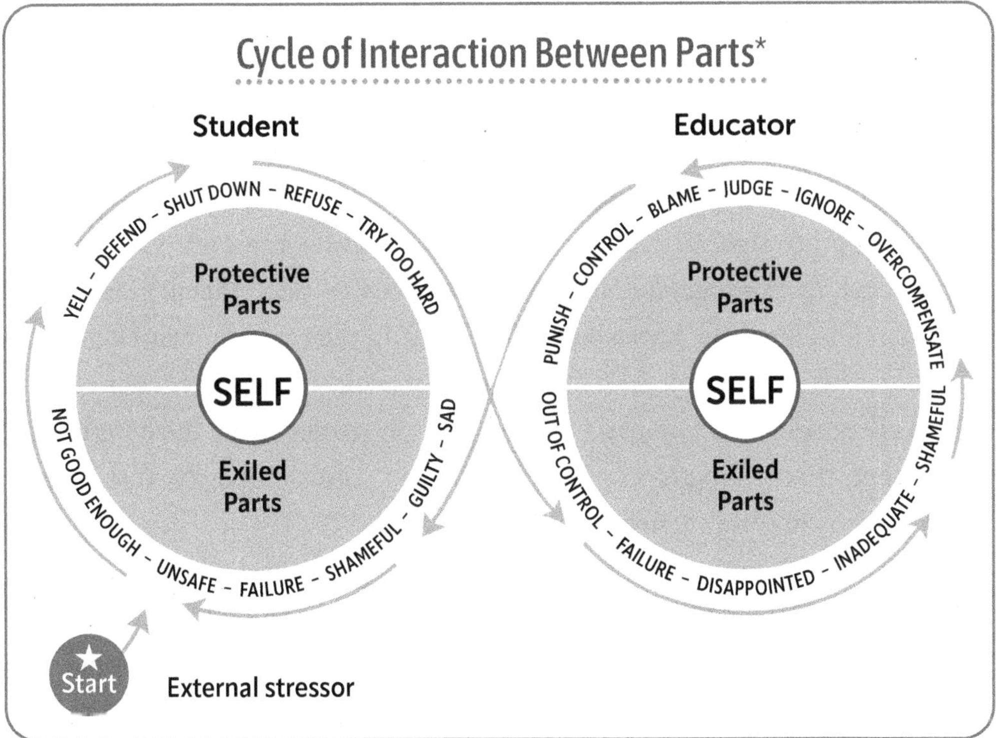

* This visual for the cycle of interaction was inspired by content from *Intimacy from the Inside Out* by Toni Herbine-Blank, Donna M. Kerpelman, and Martha Sweezy.

To further explain this process, let's track what happens between students and teachers over the course of a day. To begin, recall that children wake up in a variety of home situations and circumstances. All of this informs the state of the child and what parts of them we greet as they arrive at school. Many arrive each day with secret, undercover parts that may feel vulnerable—perhaps feeling sad, bad, like a failure, or out of control. Their internal system instinctively exiles these feelings, as they generally aren't safe to display. So, they come in to school with protective parts presenting on top, saying or enacting different messages such as:

- "I'm trying to be good."
- "I don't care. I'm not interested."
- "I can't do this. I refuse to try."
- "I won't follow directions."
- "I'm funny."

These (and many more) are just parts of our students, but in the moment, that's what we educators see, and so the dance begins.

What do the students' parts activate in us, the educator? As a fellow human, an educator's nervous system can detect cues if the student is feeling threatened and acting protective. The educator will instinctively respond. This may be proportional, appropriate, helpful, and customized to that student's need. Left to unconscious instincts, however, an exiled part in the educator may be touched off underneath—a part that feels disrespected, inadequate, or out of control. This in turn energizes protective parts in the educator: parts playing the hero to save the student, parts trying to dominate and regain control, or parts that use the strategy of turning away to avoid failure.

The educator's protective response, then, may further exacerbate the student. For example, if the student interprets that the educator thinks they are different, incapable, or problematic, this touches off further feelings of vulnerability in the child and even greater protective parts. A cycle begins to play out. The core dynamic at play here is that protective parts activate protective parts. It's a basic survival mechanism: As we receive and send cues of fight, flight, freeze, or fawn to one another, we each put the other on guard. Protectors energize and polarize each other, only escalating the situation and all the while thinking they are acting in our best interests. There is a great irony in this. As protector parts activate and escalate protective reactions in others, it creates disconnection; parts instinctively wall off, hide out, separate, and feel even more alone. The student's protective responses are trying to secure safety and reassurance that they are good; instead, they get the opposite. Meanwhile, the educator's protective responses want to ensure they are helping, getting things under control, and motivating the student; the educator also gets the exact opposite of what they wanted.

Now that we've seen how this plays out in a one-on-one interaction, let's recognize what this means in a classroom where a teacher is simultaneously responding to multiple children and all their different parts. As the teacher juggles responses to each student's needs, the teacher may feel as though they are constantly shifting into different parts of themselves, as if forever changing costumes or masks. This may be further amplified if multiple students arrive each morning coming from challenging or even traumatic situations, nervous systems already on alert. And what if the teacher had a rough morning too, and their protector parts are already on guard? Myriad signals can fly fast, activating concerns about safety, perception of threat, and need for protection. In addition, it may be that all these protector parts got activated outside of school and remain on duty in school, not registering the change of circumstance. All this and it is only 8:30 in the morning! Imagine how exhausting this cycle can become for the educator and the students.

Parts-Led Interactions vs. Self-Led Interactions

In order to grasp how this cycle plays out, the next two sections are going to reflect on an interaction between a teacher and a student, first led by protective parts (i.e., part-to-part), and then driven by Self-led parts (i.e., heart-to-heart). As you read through both scenarios, track the different parts in the teacher and student, seeing how they activate each other in a reactive sequence.

PART-TO-PART INTERACTIONS

Before Jesse left home, her mother accused her of not remembering to take out the trash and added, "You never remember what you are supposed to do. How did I get such an absent-minded, careless child?" Feeling sad, inadequate, and not good enough, Jesse arrived at school. Of course, she wanted to keep these feelings secret, so she donned a part to feel safe.

Jesse entered class with her "be good" protector on top. She quietly sat down, determined to be focused and try her best. Jesse's teacher, Ms. D., appreciated this cooperative start to the day and reinforced Jesse's behavior, saying, "Nice behavior. I wish I saw this more often." However supportive this was meant to be, it only reinforced Jesse's story about herself—that she's not good enough.

After 30 minutes of struggling with a math problem that didn't make sense to her, Jesse raised her hand and asked for help. Ms. D., tired from weeks of Jesse not successfully engaging, responded with irritation: "Well, you must not have been listening during the lesson when I explained it. Read the directions on the top of the worksheet."

Jesse then felt even worse about herself and wanted to give up. She put her head down, trying another protective strategy. Ms. D. saw this and felt bad. This energized an "I'll do anything to encourage my student" part to approach Jesse, saying, "Come on, Jesse. Don't give up. You can do this!"

Jesse interpreted this as a message that she was not trying hard enough. She couldn't stand it anymore and erupted at Ms. D., saying, "Math is so dumb! You are a terrible teacher!"

With this, Ms. D. felt hurt, which prompted her to blame Jesse: "That's it. I've been more than patient and helpful with you. If you can't behave yourself, you can go to the principal's office."

Jesse felt ashamed, taking in the message that she was bad, different, and maybe hopeless. She deflated and apologized, trying to reestablish some sense of connection. Ms. D, feeling hopeless, turned her back to ignore Jesse. It was too painful to engage, so Ms. D. put up a protective wall as she dialed for the school resource officer to come take Jesse to the office.

In this *part-to-part* interaction, Jesse's parts and the parts of Ms. D. activated one another. The following image shows another version of the cycle of interaction that transpires between teacher and student parts. Note how the activated parts bounce back and forth between parties, seemingly starting a "table tennis match" between them.

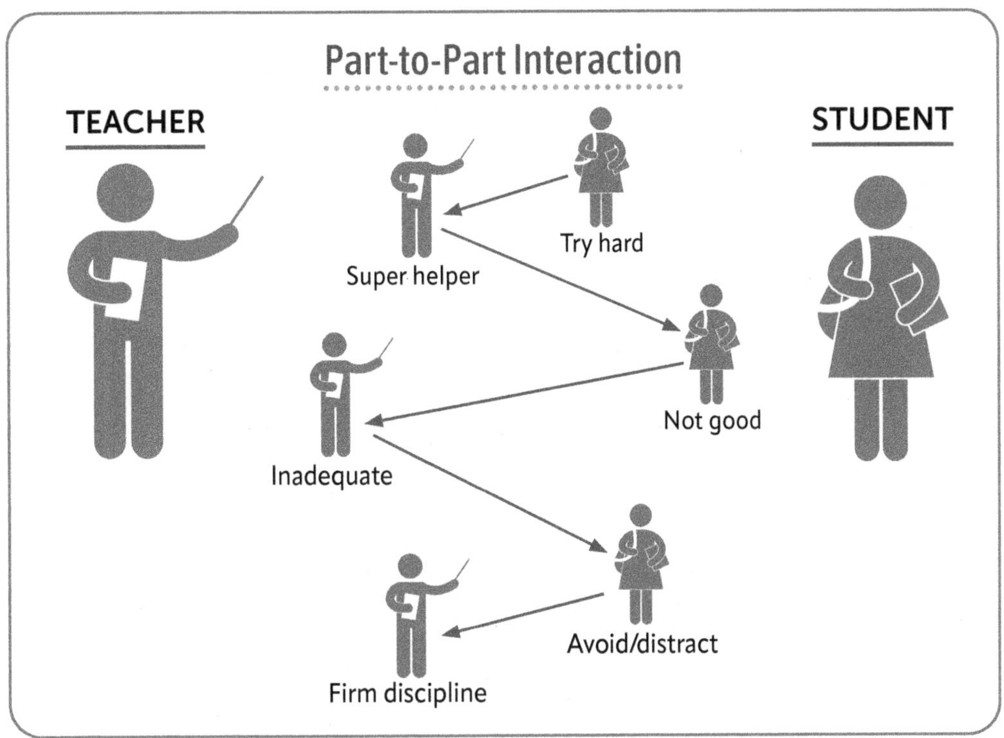

HEART-TO-HEART INTERACTION

Before Jesse left home, her mother accused her of not remembering to take out the trash and added, "You never remember what you are supposed to do. How did I get such an absent-minded, careless child?" Feeling sad, inadequate, and not good enough, Jesse showed up for class quiet, her gaze downcast.

Ms. D. greeted her at the door to check in. "How are you doing today? Thumbs up or thumbs down?" When Jesse turned her thumb down, Ms. D. pointed to the feelings map on the wall and asked, "You want to name what's up?"

Jesse looked at it for a moment and pointed to *discouraged*. Then, after a moment, she pointed to *determined*. She explained, "I just feel like I am never good enough. But . . . I'll try my best today, I promise."

Recognizing the voice of a manager part, Ms. D. responded, "Jesse, it's okay. I get it's one of those days when some parts of you are struggling. What do you need?"

Jesse replied, "Space."

Ms. D. acknowledged this, saying, "Okay. That's fair. Just know I'm here for you if I can help."

Jesse felt reassured and went to her desk. In a sense, what she needed most was what she received: acceptance.

Once the class was settled, Ms. D. started into a new math lesson. Anticipating this might activate a few of her students, she gave them a heads-up. "Today, we are going to start some new material. There are aspects of this that can seem a bit tricky. Parts of you may even feel confused or frustrated for a bit as we try this. Just remember that all these responses are normal. We can slow it down as much as needed and break it into bite-size pieces. If you have any questions, ask. You will get this."

Jesse patiently listened and followed the lesson, and then started into her work. Fifteen minutes into the handout, she still felt it didn't make sense. Everyone else was peacefully working. She thought, *See, something is wrong with me. No matter how hard I try, I'm still not good enough.* She put her head on the desk, ready to give up.

Ms. D. noticed a feeling of helplessness and frustration rise up inside her as she noticed Jesse. Ms. D. stopped to take a breath, ask those parts to step back, and reconnect with confidence. She then slowly approached Jesse, bent down to the student's level and, in a quiet, private voice, asked, "Hey, Jesse, looks like this is tough for you. I'd like to understand what's going on. Let me know if you want to talk." Ms. D. paused at the desk for a moment in silence. When Jesse didn't respond, Ms. D. walked away.

Within three minutes, Jesse lifted her head and quietly walked to her teacher's desk to request assistance. Jesse explained, "I just feel so stupid. I want to give up."

Ms. D. acknowledged Jesse, saying, "I hear you. It makes sense that a part of you wants to give up. This is hard right now. And when you put your head down, it seems like that's another part of you trying to help you take a break and get some space. Is that right?"

Jesse nodded in agreement, then said, "You know, I was actually doing fine until I got to question 5. Can you just explain that to me?" Ms.. D. patiently explained the concept again, in a new way that Jesse could understand. Reassured, Jesse returned to her desk. Both teacher and student moved on, feeling accomplished and connected.

In this *heart-to-heart* interaction, Jesse and Ms. D. were able to connect from Self when Ms. D. unblended, cared for her own parts, and then recognized and cared for the parts she detected in her student. As Ms. D. was more Self-led, her interaction called forth greater Self-leadership in Jesse. In the following image, we can see how leading from Self allows both parties to deescalate, build connection, and lead to productive engagement with the situation at hand.

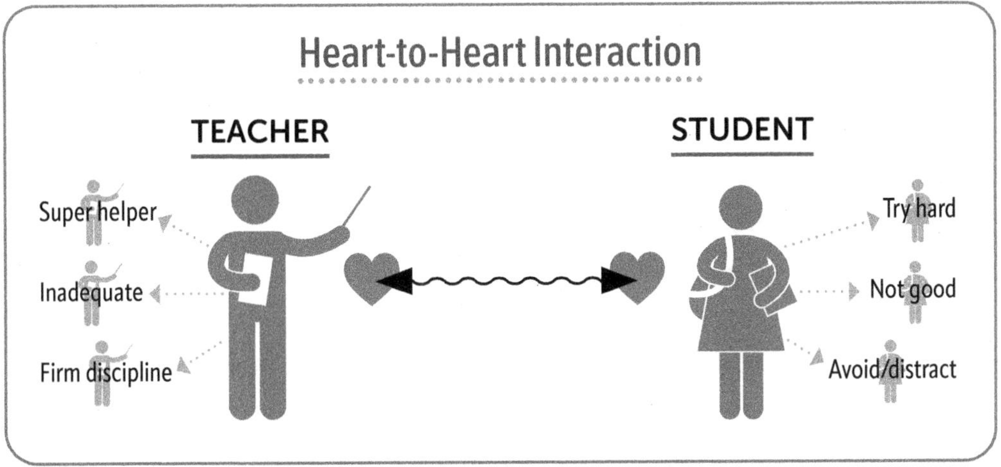

Shifting from Parts-Led to Self-Led

In any interaction, if one person notices they are letting a protective part lead and they take a moment to unblend from this part and rest back into Self, they have the power to shift the dynamic as a whole. It only takes one person to pause. As adults, we often identify the students' behaviors as the problem and see them as the primary people who need to make a shift. As adults, however, we generally have more power to be self-aware, take greater perspective, and exhibit more self-control and skill to be the first person to step back. Even when a student is highly dysregulated, we have the power to send a countersignal that moves both parties toward greater connection, clarity, and resolution. In doing so, we shift from part-to-part interactions to heart-to-heart interactions. If adults have the courage to recognize their contribution to the interaction, they can regulate their own system and approach the student with true curiosity and compassion. From this place, the student can be coached in a new way to process their emotions and express themselves productively (think of the RISE model).

The *U* of PAUSE: Understanding Each Other to Nurture Self-Led Relationships

Humans are wired for connection—we are meant to be here for each other. We need each other not only to survive but to thrive. When we can optimize our power to connect with each other, we create a zone in which we can feel seen, known, valued, celebrated, encouraged, witnessed, and cherished. With each other, we have the opportunity to remember and call forth the essential nature, the core goodness and unique value in each precious human. Holding the conviction of the Self at everyone's core and leaning into compassionate awareness of parts, we are equipped with the tools to realize the transformative power inherent in everyday relationships.

How then do we practically apply our knowledge of Self and parts to cultivate healthy, nourishing relationships? Let's break down the practical skills we can integrate in our daily interactions to nurture connection. These skills are reflected in the *U* of the PAUSE model, which stands for *understanding* each other. Having taken time to connect to Self and develop awareness, we are already more Self-led and ready to place our attention on others, to be curious where they are coming from, to listen and "get" them, and also to share our experience in a calm, clear way so others can receive our perspective.

There are three essential aspects for healthy, Self-led interactions:

1. **Being the Self in the system:** Unblending from and befriending our parts to show up as our optimal Self in interactions
2. **Listening from Self:** Listening so everyone feels welcomed, their parts feel heard, and they are seen as their whole Self (not just parts)
3. **Speaking for parts:** Effectively representing our parts to each other so we appreciate each other's different perspectives and needs

Be the Self in the System

Even as we focus on calling forth the best in our students, so much of empowering them ultimately comes back to us, the adults caring for them. The more we cultivate our awareness of when we are in Self and our capacity to shift back into Self when parts take over, the more we are able to show up, moment to moment, for our students' needs. As we stay centered, we are the eye of the storm, the *Self in the system*.

While students enter school with many different parts driving their behavior, we can practice maintaining calm, effective leadership for the class. As we approach students, their parts can feel the 8 C qualities of Self emanating from us: calm, compassion, courage, curiosity, confidence, clarity, creativity, and connection. When authentically embodied, the presence of these qualities is contagious. Students pick up cues that the environment is safe, their protectors step down, and they respond by being more centered, relaxed, and open. With time, this spreads to the whole class and creates a Self-led container for all students' nervous systems, helping them regulate and engage from the moment they enter school. As the majority of students shift to being relatively more in Self—present, connected, and engaged—there is an overall increase of Self in the system. Even the students with the most extreme protector parts feel the effect and are supported to reconnect when they get triggered. Our Self-leadership serves as the central tuning fork for the system, rather than the influence of the more extreme parts in students.

As we hold the intention to act as the Self in the system, we continue to operate with the conviction that Self is present within all our students, giving them the capacity to function optimally. One goal of this model is for students to know how to access Self-leadership for themselves and thus recognize and attend to their own parts. As we know, some students are already wired to operate from pretty extreme parts and may, at least initially, struggle to access Self. As we relate to students and their parts from Self, the student gradually internalizes our words and approach. Eventually, they grow the capacity to pause, hold self-compassion, and lead *themselves* and their own parts through tough experiences. Therefore, in the context of everyday interactions with us, students can learn and integrate the essence of emotional intelligence, resilience, and how to be a healthy human being. In addition to our influence on students, we, as adults in the system, have a profound and continuous effect on each other and the overall climate of the school. As we practice being more Self-led, our very presence can be calming, comforting, or inspiring to others, including our fellow educators. Therefore, even one person in a school community who consciously cultivates Self-leadership can dramatically shift the trajectory of interactions, model a new way of relating, and have a ripple effect on community well-being. We should not underestimate the power of Self-leadership!

Learning to be the Self in the system is a substantial and lifelong endeavor that hinges on a simple daily practice: building the awareness of what is happening within us and resting into Self, over and over again. It might look something like this: We start the day with an intention or perhaps self-reflection practice. As we get caught up in the day, our parts get activated; as a result, our attention wanders, our mood shifts, and perhaps we overreact. Then we *pause*, reset, and—now back in touch with our intention—we set out again to lead from Self. Later in the day, several students are behaving from extreme parts just as our administrator comes to observe us! Once again, our parts are activated as the situation appears out of control and overwhelming. Just as before, we *pause*, step back, take a breath—being *aware* of our parts—and draw up one of the qualities of Self, such as curiosity. We bring this quality to the situation at hand, *understanding* our students' needs.

Success is not defined by operating from a perfect Self-led state at all times. Rather, success is defined by a moment-to-moment practice; in one interaction at a time, we notice a part has taken over, *pause* to remember Self, become *aware* of our parts, position ourselves to *understand*, and start again. This repetition builds our "muscle" to be Self-led. And in this practice of shifting into Self over and again, we show students how to do it too. We give them permission to have their many parts and demonstrate the option to practice returning to Self.

Listening from Self

The foundation for collaborative action is effective communication. When things go poorly in our interactions or relationships, we frequently attribute it to a breakdown in communication: a misunderstanding, incorrect assumptions, or crossed wires. Sound familiar? This happens because communication can be quite a parts party—a chaotic conversation without a leader. To lead from Self in our everyday relationships, we must learn to listen from Self.

We can tell when someone is truly listening to us. Often, our body relaxes and settles. Perhaps we don't feel so alone, or our own thinking clarifies and we even recognize what we need, what matters to us, or what we wish we could do, all because someone listened. With students, one of the most powerful and profound gifts we can offer is our listening. When we listen, they discover their inner experience, name their emotions, identify their unique ideas, and build confidence in their knowing. In the act of true deep listening, we make space for Self, encourage creative ideas, and foster a sense of knowing. This intimate, welcoming exchange is at the heart of learning and can be the pinnacle of shared human experience.

Pause and Reflect

- Can you recall a moment when you felt really heard and understood?
- What did that feel like in your body? What else happened inside of you as a result of being heard?
- What did the listener do that worked for you?

LAYERS OF LISTENING

To discover how to effectively listen, we will consider the layers of listening. The outer ring is the "me" level, when our listening is actually all about "me"—our thoughts and feelings. The second ring is the "you" level, the level where our purpose and focus is on another person, wanting to understand where they are coming from. And, finally, the inner level is "us," the level at which we hold "me" *and* "you" and the situation as a whole to listen to the heart of the matter. Let's unpack each level of listening.

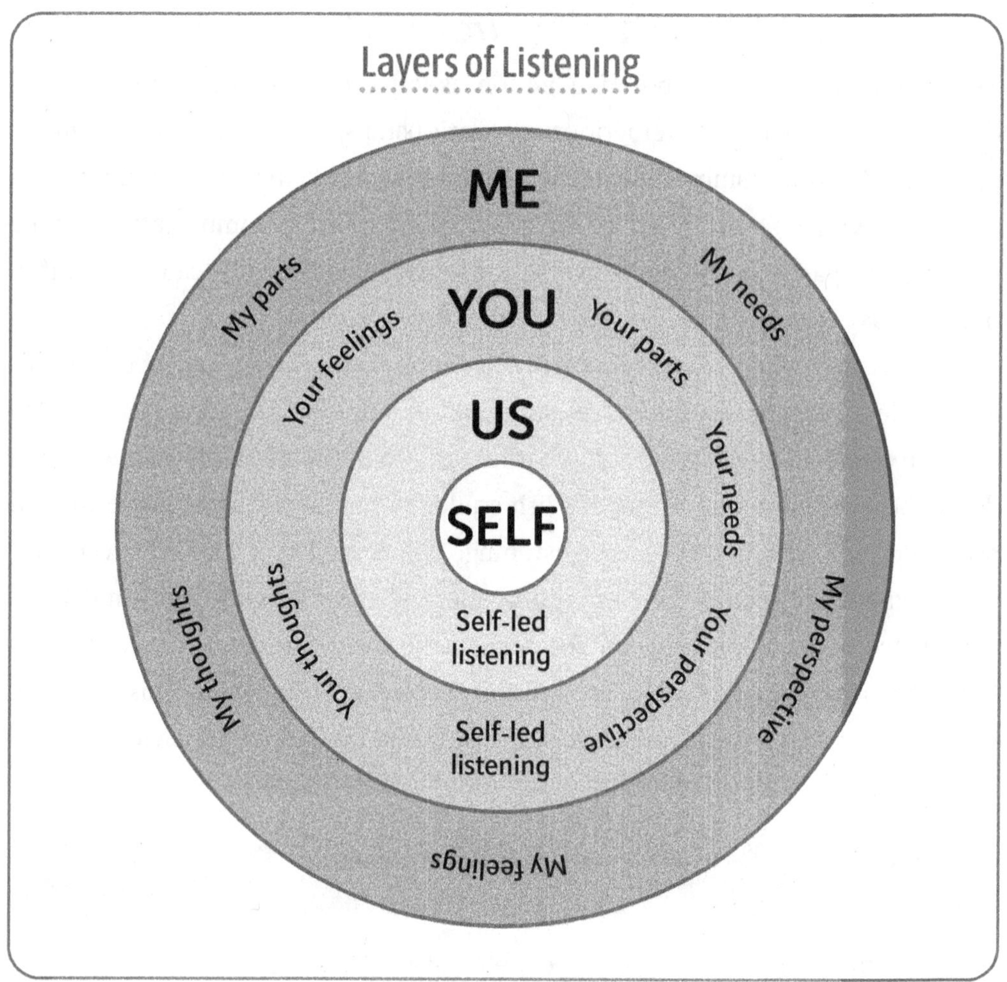

ME-LEVEL LISTENING

Even when we're aware of the power of listening, we often don't really know how to listen or don't realize when we've stopped listening. We can probably all bring to mind someone who is *not* a good listener. They might only talk about themselves, and if they ask us a question, they don't pay attention to the answer. For example, consider that neighbor or relative at a holiday party. They ask you, "What's new?" and you start to share about your new job, only to have them interrupt to tell you about their latest work project.

Now, if we are honest with ourselves, we probably can also acknowledge moments when we were listening to someone else, got distracted, then came back to listening, embarrassed by what we missed. This is what it looks like when parts are running the show.

As we've explored in the cycle of interaction, when someone shares with us, especially if they are in distress or struggling with a problem (i.e., acting from a protector part), our parts can get activated too. If someone says to us, "I'm overwhelmed and can't handle this . . ." our ideal first step is to notice our impulse to react. Very often, this impulse comes from a protector part of our own. One simple way to tell whether we are reacting from Self or a part is to notice our agenda: where we are coming from. For example, we can consider if we're coming from one of the following agendas:

- Help, fix, or solve
- Judge, assess, figure out, or be right
- Comfort, rescue, or take the pain away
- Defend, blame, or shame others
- Shut down and push away
- Other

While well-intentioned, these parts are generally more about us wanting to feel relief or reassurance that we are a good person. This way of listening to others is actually "all about *me*!"

YOU-LEVEL LISTENING

To access a bit more Self in your listening process, you can ask your parts to step back. How do you do this? While listening, you can notice your running inner commentary and impulse to jump in. This chatter is simply the voice of parts. See if you can invite these protective parts with a need to react to soften and rest back for a few minutes so you can just listen. Another way to do this may be through your body. You can check for physical cues as you listen: Is there tension, energy bursting to act, or a sense of drive? Again, these are often signs of parts. One way to reconnect to your center is to notice your breath and feel your feet on the ground. As you do this, you may notice some of the 8 C qualities rise up. This is a good sign you are more available to be with the other person.

With connection to Self, you are ready to show up and focus on the other person. How then can you truly listen—that is, not only hear what they are saying but also let them feel that you get them?

- To begin, allow your body language to convey the idea that "I am here with you." Find an open posture and place your gaze on them.
- Tune into the other person's ideas, feelings, physical cues, experiences, and needs. This is the next layer of listening—all about *them*.
- Ask open-ended questions to support exploration and clarification of their experience.
- Reflect back what you understand: "What I hear you saying is . . ."

You do not need to be an expert in interpreting what they say, and you don't have to agree with their thoughts or feelings. Rather, you are simply there to keep company and witness their experience. In fact, we can typically offer more to someone else if we stay anchored in our Self and don't blend with their feelings. You can be a "parts detector" to notice and differentiate various parts as they speak, as well as a "Self detector" to see the signs of their core Self ever-present amid the play of parts. By being in Self, we offer another person the gift of validating their story of their parts while ultimately calling forth their authentic Self.

What is the effect of Self-led listening? It makes other people's parts feel more safe and able to settle, allowing the person to rest into Self. When parts assert themselves strongly or loudly, it is because they have a message to convey. Listening sends a direct message to parts—"I get you"—which allows them to feel acknowledged, deescalate, and unblend. Feeling heard supports the other person in witnessing their inner experience and discovering their own insights about what might be possible. Listening fosters connection and mutual acceptance that creates a foundation upon which to move into *us-level listening*—that is, listening to the heart of the matter and understanding what is needed for all involved.

While Self-led listening often unfolds intuitively when we access the qualities of Self, we may sometimes engage with some pretty intense or complex dynamics with others. Following the steps of U-BAC can offer a familiar framework for us to see and relate to parts in someone else. The following table offers prompts to apply the U-BAC steps that can be applied during Self-led listening. (Please see this as a menu of cues you can draw from rather than a rigid process to follow.)

U-BAC for Listening to Others

Unblend	Ask, "What's up? How are you right now?" • Be a parts detector. • Remember you are listening to parts in someone else and remember Self in their core. • Reflect back the signals of parts: thoughts, feelings, sensations. "It seems like you are feeling pretty tense about this situation. Do I get it?" • Notice specific parts, possibly using parts language: "I get that a part of you is super frustrated about this situation. Is that right?"
Befriend	Say, "Help me understand where you are coming from." • Be curious about the *message* from the person's different parts, their perspectives, and where they are coming from. • Listen for their motive and mission: their positive intent and main fears or concerns. • Check your understanding: "It seems like a part of you is trying hard to communicate and you're worried you aren't being understood. Am I getting it?"
Attend	Ask, "What do you need? How can I help you right now?" • Directly or indirectly, inquire about the 4 As: acceptance, appreciation, assurance, or assistance. • Wonder about needs you detect: "It sounds like you need more clarity on our plans and you need to know you don't have to do this alone. Does that sound right?"
Connect	When we are connected to our parts, we connect with one another and to the heart of the moment. As we cycle through unblending, befriending, and attending during a conversation, the natural result is that another person's parts feel seen and gotten, supporting them to relax. This in turn creates space to connect. In the context of listening, there isn't anything to do here except notice the signs of connection.

Keep in mind as you embark on unblending that it may or may not work to explicitly ask another person about their parts. That is okay—if you remember that the other person has multiple parts, you will start to notice as they shift between the voices and perspective of these different parts, and you can remember that their core Self is always there. Befriending happens as you get curious to understand where the other person is coming from. Finally, as you tune into what they need, you are attending, which creates space for natural connection.

I experienced the power of this listening model as a school-based community therapist when I was called to work with Thomas, a junior in high school who was struggling to maintain passing grades. Thomas was a quiet, gentle young man who started the meeting by expressing his sadness and shame that he couldn't do better in school. He assured me he really wanted to succeed but couldn't.

I acknowledged the part of him that was committed to putting in the effort for school, then asked him what happens after school when it's time to do homework. He said he just felt tired and would go to his room, curl up into blankets, and watch movies. I used parts language to reflect back the part of him who wants to do well and another part—that is sometimes dominant—that wants to retreat to his room (unblending). I then asked how going to his room helped him (befriending). He said ever since he was little, when his parents would fight, this was his way of calming down and not getting overwhelmed. I validated that this made sense and acknowledged how this part is supporting him. He was amazed, his gaze lifted, and with more energy, he asked, "So what can I do?"

"Well, it seems like they are both trying to help you with something you need: to do well in school and to have down time (attending). If you could mediate a conversation between these parts, what might be possible?"

Thomas then easily identified a plan to allocate time each day to be with each part, caring for his needs. Two weeks later, Thomas reported it was working, and miraculously, his grades were going up!

THE COURAGE TO LISTEN FIRST AND SPEAK SECOND

One of the main obstacles to Self-led listening arises when both people's parts are activated *and* both people really want to be understood and respected. In other words, both people want and need the other person to be the listener first. The question, then, is who will step back and be the listener?

When this dynamic plays out between adults, it takes great self-control to be the one to listen first. I don't mean to just be quiet, but to actually *listen*. Stepping up as the first listener requires extraordinary patience, humility, and courage. It all comes back to being in Self. If one person can step out of their agenda-driven protector parts and listen from Self, it transforms the whole experience. Both people can then listen into the whole of the situation, attuning to the needs of the moment and discerning what is truly beneficial.

When we are with students, however, we often have more capacity and maturity to wait for our turn to speak. Once the student is heard and acknowledged, their parts will relax. Then what happens? Sometimes the student offers a great solution, and sometimes they are then ready to hear our perspective. They may even reveal that they've heard our viewpoint the many other times we've said it (and we don't need to repeat our "wise words"). In the end, this approach supports students in feeling more trusted and empowered, and we often talk less (and save energy). Win-win!

Let me share an example from my experience as a parent. When my son was in middle school, he was processing many external realities: hearing about classmates vaping and trying drugs, grappling with increased demands at school, and sorting through social dynamics with friends. Sometimes this process brought strong emotional displays. While there were times I remembered the context of his experience, there were days I forgot.

For example, one day he was upset with himself for forgetting to turn in homework, which resulted in a poor overall grade. Rather than being curious to help him unpack the situation and discover what he could learn from it, I responded firmly, "Well, that's your responsibility. You need to figure out how you are going to keep track of your assignments." My "patient and accommodating" side was done and I'd moved into my "boundary-setting mama bear" part. My tone was short and judgmental. Within an instant, he escalated and stormed out of the room. I followed him and told him he needed be able to take feedback and should settle himself down. He then tossed himself on the couch, crying.

I then stepped away. Was that helpful? Was I off? I thought about my words. I was setting clear expectations and seeing him for what he was capable of . . . right? I then looked deeper. Where was I coming from? I could feel a part of me was cold and firm, distancing him. I then recognized that he was displaying a part that I also had in myself that I didn't like: the part that is sometimes forgetful or distracted or disorganized. Rather than staying connected and open-hearted to coach him through this moment, I was coming from a critical, hard side of me. No wonder he had gotten upset and escalated.

I returned to his side. I told him, "A part of me was cold and impatient a few minutes ago. I apologize because that is not the way I want to be with you. Help me understand what is happening inside you." With that, he downloaded his own thoughts and feelings about forgetting his homework. He went on to add that one of his best friends had been critical of him for being forgetful, and this led him to feel less-than. As I listened and reflected his experience back to him, I felt compassion rise up. Eventually, he settled down and told me he really wanted to be a good student. He shared what he wanted to try doing differently to keep track of his work. He had the wisdom and the answers. All he needed from me was listening.

As a parent, I frequently find that it is hardest to offer Self-led listening when I see parts in my son that I struggle with myself. While it's hard to admit (and even harder to remember in the moment), the more activated a response I have to my son, the more it indicates work *I* need to do. As I listen to and befriend my parts, I am more and more available to listen and befriend his parts. The process of seeing and attending to my own parts can be humbling and even painful at times. But learning to be gentle with myself, allowing myself to be "good enough," has proved to be the most rewarding and freeing experience as I watch it create the space for my son to flourish.

Numerous educators have reflected a similar phenomenon. Often as they debrief challenging moments, reflecting on a student's behavior and their own response, they recognize that the student reflects something in themselves. If they have trouble listening to and sitting with an anxious student, they may recognize they are not at peace with their own experience of anxious parts. If the educator quickly shuts down any expression of anger and struggles to hear its positive intent, it may be that parts of them have exiled their own anger. As they befriend these parts in themselves, they gain the capacity to stay engaged, compassionate, and constructive in guiding their students.

It's worth noting that many days, befriending and attending to our parts requires allowing ourselves to be a "good enough" educator. Like our students, we too are works in progress. When we can be patient and gentle with our own parts, it equips us to most effectively guide and care for our children.

Speaking for Parts

Pause and Reflect

- When you have strong feelings or an important idea to communicate, and you want to be understood by another, how do you communicate?
- What works for you to know others understand you?

The other essential component in communication is, of course, speaking. What are some commonplace patterns we see when people are speaking with each other? Some people feel the need to vent and download. Others hold it all in and wish to keep things private. Some want to share the whole of their story while others shift the focus away from themselves. In all these ways and more, we are seeking to understand and to be understood, and very often, we struggle with how to represent ourselves so others can hear us. Frequently, this is because we speak from our parts.

What does it mean to speak *from* parts? It means allowing our parts to directly share all their thoughts and feelings through us. We are blended and identified with a part and it is speaking through us *as* us. We might excuse ourselves: *I'm just being honest!* But depending on how intense this part is and the content of its message, its honesty may not be as well received by others as we would hope. Instead, the part's message might overwhelm others, thus activating them to either join our emotional wave or pull back and block us in order to feel safe. When this happens, we generally don't get the kind of understanding or relief that we long for.

Instead of speaking *from* parts, we can learn to speak *for* parts. When we speak for parts, we speak from a space of Self-leadership—calm, compassionate, and curious—and represent our parts. Picture yourself, the Self in the system, as the heart at the center of your team of parts and your parts gathered around you in a circle. From a place of calm, you represent your inner experience: "A part of me thinks . . ." or "Another part of me feels . . . and needs . . ." or "At the same time, a part of me appreciates that you . . ." This may seem like a minor shift in language, but it is revolutionary for our interactions. The following image shows the differences between speaking *from* a part and *for* a part. Note the differences in language between the top and bottom half, and consider how you might rephrase some statements in the top half to be more like the bottom half.

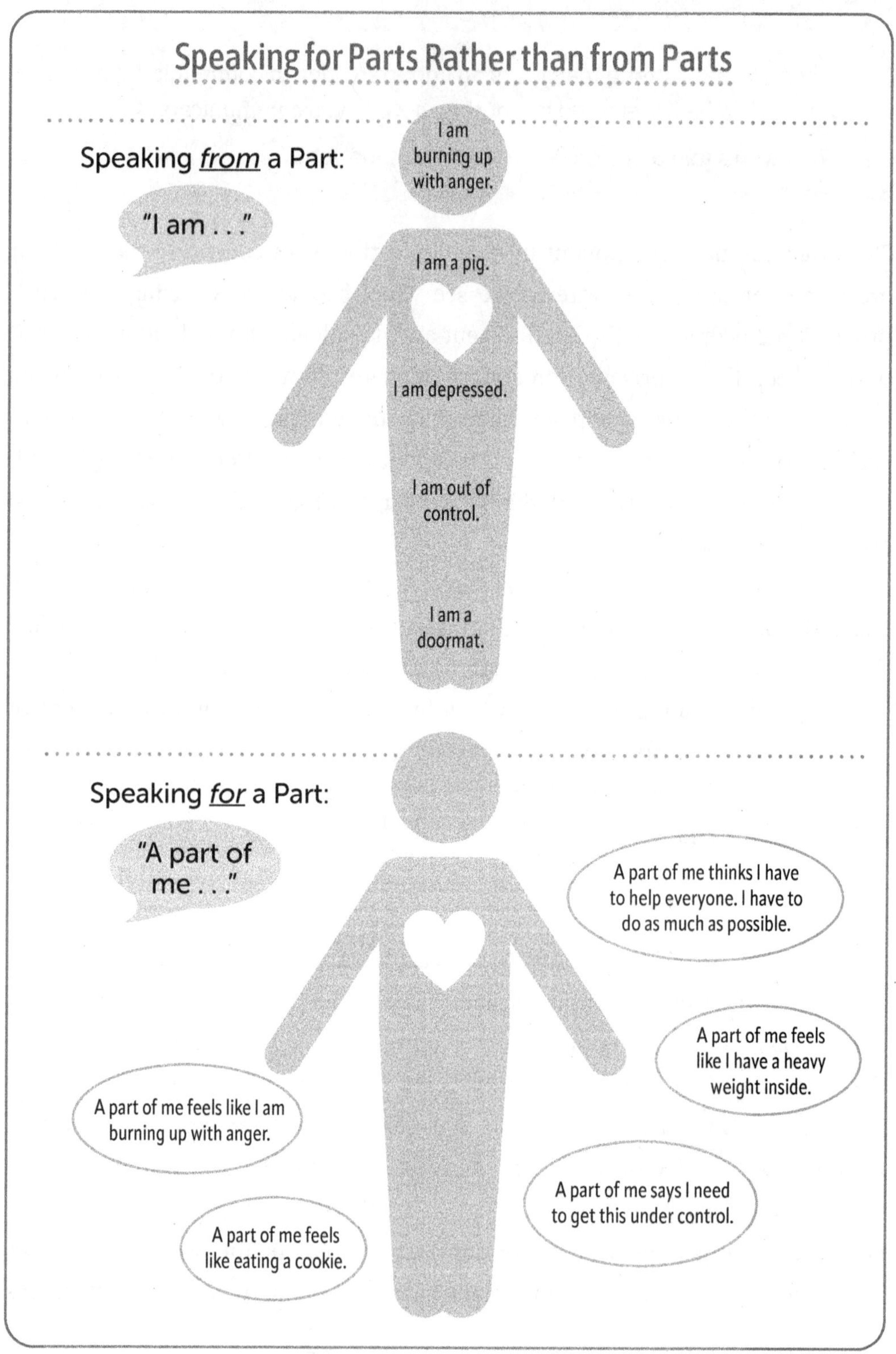

In the practice of speaking for our parts, we also build in breathing space to assess which parts are present and decide what we choose to share, considering which parts of us would experience benefit or relief if we speak for them and consciously contemplating the impact our sharing will have.

Speaking for parts builds a natural pause into communication, which benefits speaker and listener alike. In order to speak for our parts, we scan inside to consider what parts we are experiencing; then we unblend and shift into the vantage point of Self. This is similar to what is described by interpersonal neurobiologist Dr. Daniel Siegel (2012), who teaches a technique he calls "Name it to tame it"—in it, parents support children in recognizing and naming their emotions and logically telling the story of their experience. Siegel explains that when we activate "mindsight" to recognize our inner experience and name it, we utilize different areas of the brain and calm the nervous system.

Speaking from Self and for our parts also changes the experience of the interaction for the listener. The listener can more easily see the difference between the speaker and their multiple parts and receives the message from the speaker's part in a clear, accessible way. All of this makes the listener much more likely to stay calm, curious, and available to receive the speaker's message.

In a conversation in which each person speaks for their parts, we move into Self together and attend to any parts that are showing up. This makes our communication both efficient and fulfilling. It applies to teachers speaking with students and also to students speaking with other students to resolve conflict. Additionally, it eases interactions between adults, such as colleagues collaborating on a project or an administrator giving constructive feedback to a staff member. When integrated into classroom and school practice, speaking for parts and listening from Self can in and of itself transform schools.

When we speak for our parts, we can:

- **Describe our inner experience and landscape:** "A part of me is a bit unsettled, while another part is just excited about the change."
- **Represent how we have been affected:** "When you laughed at my comment, a part of me understood you thought it was funny and another part of me felt confused and a bit hurt."
- **Convey our story about a person, owning that it is just that—*our* story, not the whole story:** "A part of me has a story about you that you

really love reading and get so involved that you forget other projects. Is that right?"

- **Give context on how we are showing up and experiencing the shared space:** "While a part of me is aware of our shared priority to work efficiently on our projects, another part of me wants today to slow down our process a bit to do a careful job and think this through. "

NOTE: Be attentive to *not* use parts language as a way to blame or presume parts in others. For example, saying something like "A part of me thinks you are manipulative and attacking me" is labeling or describing the other person. This is likely to activate a protective response in them. Instead, delve deeper to go past what you think the other person did to get in touch with what *you* are feeling and experiencing inside, and then speak for these parts in you. For example, you might say something like "Right now a part of me feels like I don't have a lot of options. I also have a part that felt small when I heard your comment."

Sometimes a simple word or phrase is adequate to let others know what parts are on top for us; sometimes we need to share a bit more. Here again we can apply U-BAC as a framework to more deeply inform how we speak for parts:

- When following U-BAC as a formula in conversation, we can first differentiate from or name the part (unblending): "A part of me is feeling disappointed."
- Next, we can convey our part's message or positive intent (befriending): "This part of me was working hard for us to have a dinner party so we could have time together as a project team outside of work."
- Finally, following the attending step, we can express the part's need or request: "I recognize that I'd love to find a way to still get together. Could we work on setting another time?"

The following table includes a few sentence stems that can support you to speak for your part with another person following the U-BAC framework. These are meant as a soft guide; please adapt them with language that accurately shares your experience and needs with others. To be effective in applying U-BAC to represent your parts to another, it is recommended you take time to prepare your reflections individually before you try to communicate with another.

U-BAC for Speaking for Parts

Unblend	Speak for the part, differentiating it from you while being with it: • "A part of me thinks/feels/senses . . ." • "On the one hand, I think . . . and on the other hand, I feel . . ."
Befriend	Speak for the part, expressing its message or motive (positive intent): • "Where this part of me is coming from is . . ." • "The reason this is coming up is . . ." • "This is important to me because . . ." • "My main concern is . . ."
Attend	Speak for the part, representing its underlying need or request: • "What this part needs is . . ." • "I'd like to request that . . ."
Connect	Express acknowledgment of your listener: • "Thank you." • "This is helpful to me because . . ." • "Can you reflect back what you understand so I know if I am expressing myself clearly?"

ADULTS SPEAKING FOR THEIR OWN PARTS WITH STUDENTS

It is powerful for students to hear adults speak for their parts. Students learn by seeing their teachers model the skill; they discover they are not alone in having strong emotions and a complex inner team of parts. In witnessing an adult's effort to recognize and care for their own parts, students see an example of how to practice self-compassion and how to respond to challenges with Self-leadership. Speaking for parts also provides adults with an effective way to communicate their feelings and needs without students feeling blamed and responsible for the adult's feelings, such as: "I am seeing a number of people distracted right now. A part of me understands it's the end of the day and you want to get outside. There is another part of me that is a bit frustrated (unblending). I want to be sure we complete today's worksheets so we don't have to do them tomorrow (befriending). Can you work with me to consider what is possible here (attending)?"

It's essential to keep in mind that a portion of our inner response is always just about *us*—our unique perspective and wiring that we brought into the situation; often, it's something we have carried with us for years. For this reason, it is important that we are conscious about how and when we speak for our parts to a child. We don't want them to misconstrue that they are responsible for our emotions and our response. This is why, before we respond, we take a moment to pause, notice, acknowledge, and unblend from our own parts. Second, we can simply do an inner check, asking ourselves, *If I speak for my parts, will this benefit the student right now?*

ADULTS SPEAKING FOR THEIR PARTS WITH OTHER ADULTS

The interactions of a school day are not only between adults and students. A great deal of a school's effectiveness relies on adults having healthy relationships with one another. This is the foundation of grade-level and team meetings, subcommittee meetings, assessment processes, feedback loops to leadership, and relationships with families. Our interpersonal conversations with colleagues are like a tennis match between our parts, serving up and responding to perspectives, convictions, thoughts, and feelings.

Educators are at times uncomfortable with the idea of speaking for their parts; some insist that their feelings are private and not appropriate to bring up in a professional setting. Of course, there are necessary and healthy boundaries around how much of our inner experience we share with colleagues. At the same time, we are already revealing our parts, often unconsciously, through our tone of voice, quality of eye contact, differing opinions, and turns of phrase. The more we are conscious of this, the more we can choose to effectively represent our experience and perspective to each other by speaking for our parts. The result is adult relationships that provide genuine support, mutual understanding, and productive partnerships.

Stories from the Field

The Gift of Checking in with a Colleague

Amy Schaefer is an art teacher at a suburban public middle school in Connecticut.

It was the day before school started, and so much was up in the air. Another teacher (who has also studied Self-leadership) passed me in the hallway and quickly detected I was overwhelmed by a part. She compassionately and simply commented, "Amy, how are you doing? Seems like a part is showing up. Want to take a moment to talk about it?" It was so powerful. We spoke for less than five minutes, and by the end, I'd unblended and was ready to move forward. Without this simple check-in, I could have spent hours hijacked by this part, preoccupied and frazzled.

COACHING STUDENTS TO SPEAK FOR THEIR PARTS

As educators, we can develop our parts detector to recognize parts showing up in our students. For example, when they bring up an inner conflict, either through their words or behavior, they may naturally speak about a side of themselves, a mood, or a point of view that just takes over. To coach them through this moment of conflict, we can start reflecting their experience back to them using parts language. This both serves as reflective Self-led listening and also helps them differentiate from their part. They realize we are seeing them as a whole, complex person and that their current experience is just a part of them, not the defining whole.

We can respond with phrases like:

- "So it sounds like a part of you is feeling frustrated while another part is thinking you want to persist."
- "Wow, I get that a side of you that just wishes you could be done with this project."
- "Seems like a part of you is disappointed. Is that right?"

Please note that these phrases are exploratory in nature. The student is the only expert on their parts, so we don't assume and label their parts: "You have a part that is angry right now." If we do, that part will likely feel defensive and dig in its heels.

Students often understand and adopt parts language much more quickly than adults because they don't have as many preconceived notions and constructs about their inner lives. It could be argued that it is even more effective to introduce the language of parts in the natural flow of everyday conversation with students. As this happens, students often unconsciously adopt and reflect the language. Additionally, if it serves the situation, you can exchange the word *parts* for other synonyms; use whatever term students can best relate to, such as *side*, *aspect*, or *mode*. Review chapter 2 for more ways to describe parts to young people.

In response to our efforts to reflect a student's parts, a student might say:

- "Yeah, there is a part of me feeling . . . But on the other hand, I get that . . ."
- "Hmm, no, actually it's not that I'm feeling . . . but really a part of me just wants . . . "

These moments reveal how simple yet profound this approach can be. Using parts language is not just another thing to do. It's simply a different—and perhaps more effective and compassionate—way to engage in interactions that are already happening every day. Eventually, it's less about using parts language, and more about a shift in how we see ourselves, others, the play of well-intentioned parts, and the core Self, always there.

Community Application: Speaking for Parts, Listening from Self

In schools, we don't only interact one-on-one. In group settings, such as classes, teams, and even communities, the quality of our listening and speaking is critical to our ability to realize our purpose for being together.

Let me share an example. During the COVID-19 pandemic, I met online with entire school staff to help them process their experience. Rather than formally teaching them the idea of Self or parts, I guided a simple group process inspired by U-BAC. I started by acknowledging that with all the changes and challenges around us, we all had a lot going on inside as well; many different parts of us are probably getting activated. Next, I invited everyone to reflect on a few of the different parts they'd been feeling lately. I then prepared them to speak for these parts in small groups with a few colleagues. I invited the colleagues to listen attentively with curiosity and compassion to really understand each other. I told them there was no need to fix or give advice; the goal was just to get each other.

After sharing parts and listening in small groups, everyone returned to the large group. Scanning the faces, I saw relief, soft laughter, and even tears. When I asked about their experience, they shared how powerful it was to find out they weren't alone—that others also felt overwhelmed by the workload, worried about the kids alone at home, eager to be helpful to school leadership but also resentful that they were stretched so thin, and inadequate because no matter how hard they worked, it wasn't enough.

They went on to affirm that speaking for their parts gave them a safe way to share more honestly and discover how much they had in common. They marveled at the power of this compassionate way to listen that created the space for them to be heard in a way that most said almost never happens. Wow!

As the large group discussion continued, I asked how these parts were trying to help them (befriending). They recognized their underlying positive intentions to be good teachers, caring colleagues, responsible employees, nurturing caregivers—*and* that they were exhausted. When asked what they needed (attending), they simply said, "More of this!" They recognized that listening to and caring for each other with this authenticity allowed them to access the inner resources to continue.

Conclusion

In this chapter, we have considered how to be conscious in our relationships with others, nurture mutual understanding, and access Self for effective communication. Authentic relationships are the foundation from which students trust teachers, teachers feel respected by administrators, and community members can welcome each other's different perspectives and needs as we discover how to work together leading our learning communities.

If you find yourself connecting now with parts of yourself that are concerned about what impact you have had on children in the past, this is okay. As adults, we are works in progress. In fact, often the most valuable gift we can give children is the opportunity for them to witness us make a mistake or accidentally hurt someone, then take responsibility and make a repair. It is not possible for life to be a string of perfect interactions, perfect decisions, and perfect products. It *is* possible to practice engaging consciously, compassionately, and responsibly. As we do this, children discover that they can do it, too. In this way we nurture students with inherent, authentic resilience, not just in the face of external stressors but also in engaging with the complex nuance of human relationships. As we nurture a generation's healthy relational skills, they will gain the power to work productively and take meaningful action.

Stories from the Field

A View from a School Psychologist's Office

Julie Faude is a lower school psychologist and also works in private practice in Pennsylvania.

As a clinical psychologist working in a lower school for 25 years, my experience of helping others had been radically transformed by my immersion in IFS and by the clear-as-day practices that are a signature aspect of the PAUSE model. It has been a revelation to know how to take care of my own dear, activated parts *first* before approaching others, even under conditions at school where things happen rapid fire! As I take care of my parts first (self-regulate with kindness), I am no longer driven to quell, judge, or quiet down a behavior I'm encountering in others. Instead, after I become unblended from my "doing and fixing" parts, I simply feel curious about others' parts and what those parts are trying to achieve on behalf of the person in pain.

Through *PAUSE* practices like self-reflection and "A" practices to unblend from my parts, I am ready for "U" to understand others. By being present, I can facilitate a relationship between a person's Self and their parts, a non-pathologizing relationship of trust. I try to keep in mind that I do not know more than the person in front of me about what they need, what their story is, and what specific solution will make it "just right" for the part of them suffering. This has been a liberating change for me. The answers are not within me, but rather, they are right there in the part exhibiting the disruptive behavior. When people exhibit intense behaviors, it makes sense that this is a manifestation of a blended part going to extremes to do its job—and this part knows what it needs. I am constantly in awe of the power and good intentions of "troubling" parts, and by following the steps of PAUSE, I have learned to lovingly accept the present and whatever these parts offer.

Here's an example of following U-BAC with a student:

Tommy, a first grader, is brought to my office, crying, red-faced, eyes wide open, and looking up at me imploringly. He and another boy argued on the playground when they couldn't agree on whose turn it was to use the swings. While one of the boys settled easily, Tommy was still very upset.

Unblending: Seeing how physically dysregulated this little boy was, my priority was to help him settle physically and get a little breathing space from a part of him that had taken over. As we sat in our chairs, I made sure to give myself a breath and to feel my feet grounded on the floor. When I invited Tommy to take a breath with me, he got upset and turned away. Rather than forcing the issue (my grounding helped), I did the opposite. I acknowledged him for knowing he needed some space. I validated that a lot had happened and that the feelings he was having probably made sense. With this, I saw him take a long exhale, and he slowly turned his body to partially face me. I could tell he had unblended a little bit, was breathing more calmly, and seemed to feel safer to explore. I was *connecting* with him and his parts.

I then wondered about his experience, the part of him that was "on top." I asked, "Is there a part of you that's really frustrated because what happened on the swing set was unfair?"

Tommy nodded and added, "Yes . . . it just stinks that I always end up going last. Sometimes I don't feel like I have any friends."

"So I get there is a part feeling really frustrated and also maybe a part underneath feeling rather sad?"

He nodded.

Befriending: Now that we both recognized the parts of him that had taken over, I wanted to support Tommy to *befriend* the upset part and be curious about its intention.

"I can get why strong feelings came up for you. I picture that big response was a part of you yelling, 'Hey, I want a turn on the swings too.'"

With this, his body softened even more, and he turned to fully face me. He looked up at me with sadness and sweetness. He explained his part even more. "Yes. Sometimes I just feel so much like I want to be included. One day, I wish somebody would turn to me and say, 'Hey Tommy, you want to take a turn first?'"

I replied, simply to acknowledge. "I get that. I can imagine that if I were in your shoes, I would have a part that would feel that way too." You should have seen the way his entire body shifted and settled. Befriending allowed us to *connect* even more with his parts.

Attending: "So what do you need right now?" I asked.

Tommy was quiet for a minute. "I don't know . . . I guess I wish the other kids could learn to be nicer."

This gave me an idea. Each week I had a chance to go into his class to lead an exercise about how we get along. I told him that I had a great storybook about how kids could learn to share at recess. They could even learn some new group games! I assured him that we could discuss and practice this as a class without anyone knowing it had been an idea that came from our conversation. Together, we set the plan in motion. Tommy wanted to include "acting it out" (role-playing) and having time for the class to draw their parts at play on an iPad. It was a plan made side-by-side with an engaged and empowered partner. He returned to class ready to learn and feeling *connected* to himself and others.

Invitations to Practice

REFLECT: *Sharing Qualities of Self with Others*

Start by taking a moment to connect with the space of Self inside you. As you breathe, picture the air flowing in and out of your heart space, allowing your attention to settle inside your core. Remember the qualities of Self (calm, compassion, courage, curiosity, connection, creativity, clarity, confidence) and notice if you can detect them inside, right now, even a little bit. Breathe into this space.

Now bring to mind someone you care for. Imagine them standing in front of you. Notice how you feel toward them. Picture that you can open your heart space and share the qualities of Self with this person. Watch them respond as they feel your appreciation for them—they know you care.

Now picture someone in front of you that you feel a bit of tension or conflict with right now. Notice how you feel toward them. Recognize your responses as parts. Ask if these parts would be willing to step back. Experiment with sharing qualities of Self with them, again opening your heart space. Picture them receiving this gift from you. How do they respond?

Notice how you feel inside right now having pictured sharing Self qualities with others. Consider what it will be like next time you see these people. How might it impact your next interaction?

WRITE: *Reflect on Relationships*

- **Anticipate parts:** As you prepare to see certain people, engage in conversations that might be difficult, or teach a challenging lesson, anticipate what parts might get energized in other people. What concerns or perceptions might they enter with? What parts might be activated by the interaction or situation?
- **U-BAC:** Continue to practice U-BAC for your own parts, especially as parts of you are activated in relationships. Hold the U-BAC framework internally as you speak for your parts to others, and listen to understand others and their parts.

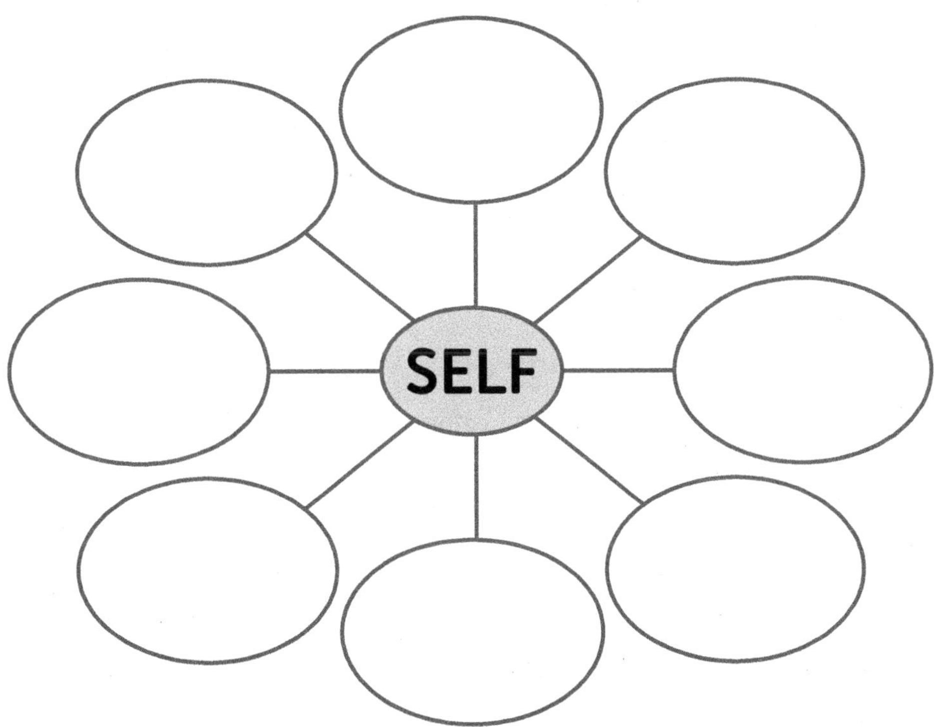

ACT: *Apply Awareness of Self and Parts in Relationships*

- **Practice being the Self in the system:** Explore how you can come back to your Self and share qualities of Self in interactions. Note the results and impact.
- **Parts detector:** Wear your parts detector at school and at home. Notice when other people shift into different parts. Be curious about their part's positive intent.
- **Integrate parts language:** Be more intentional about using parts language in your natural everyday conversations with others. Speak for your parts. Wonder or ask about their parts: "Is there a part of you that . . . ?" or "I wonder if a side of you is feeling . . ." Be careful not to assume you have the right name or understanding of their parts, such as saying, "You have a part that is angry and you need to get it under control!" Remember, you can always use synonyms for parts—the point is to notice and name our multiple sides.
- **Listen from Self:** Let yourself off the hook. Sometimes you don't need to fix, control, or direct. Just rest back, listen to understand, and recognize the underlying need.

EMBODY: *Our Body as Support in Relationship*

When you are in conversations with different people, notice changes in your body. Perhaps you lean forward or backward, cross your legs, or tilt your head. Internally, you might be aware of tension or numbness; perhaps you feel the temperature become warmer or cooler. Consider how these physical signals may reflect parts of you responding to the interaction. Perhaps parts of you feel small and other parts want to be big; some parts want to look harmless while other parts want to explode. Our body gives us extraordinary information about our relationships—cues we can learn to respect as part of our internal parts detector.

CHAPTER 4

Search for Solutions and Experiment for Self-Led Action

Pause and Reflect

- Consider some actions you have taken while in Self. Think back to a time when:
  - You acted with *confidence* and *courage*, taking a difficult but necessary action
  - You were *calm* and *clear* about making the right choice
  - You were in the flow, *creative* and *connected*, at the right place at the right time
  - You felt *compassion* to help another to choose what was most beneficial, even if it wasn't easy
- What is your experience of acting from Self-leadership? What difference do you notice in how you feel and behave in these moments? What do you see as the outcome in these moments and your effect on others?

When you walk into a school, what is happening? Students are listening, speaking, reading, reflecting, exploring, creating, and expressing. Teachers are at the board presenting new material, individually mentoring students, facilitating discussions, or leading groups of students through activities. So many other critical players—administrators, counselors, and staff—are engaged in strategizing, planning, mediating, coordinating, and responding to the needs of the moment.

In short, people are in action.

What is the quality of this action? What gives it meaning and value? How do people effectively work together when in action? Moment to moment, how do we choose what action to take?

The answers to these questions are critical in determining our ability to succeed in our mission for students to learn. Depending on where we are coming from (our parts) and how we are operating (connection to Self), our actions can either advance learning and uplift the school community *or* detract from learning and hurt the community. This is where our work to cultivate social intelligence and emotional resourcefulness can meaningfully translate into the everyday actions we take. This is where we discover that Self-leadership is the portal to optimal engagement in all aspects of school activity, unlocking our power as students and adults to be productive, innovative, and collaborative.

The concepts and skills for Self-leadership that we have discussed in the previous chapters have emphasized how we are *being*: building awareness of our parts and where we are coming from, listening to understand each other, and accessing greater Self-leadership together. Now we will consider how we practice and apply this conscious way of *being* to what we are *doing* throughout the school day so we can realize the benefits of Self-leadership in everyday action.

In this chapter, we will:

- Explore how parts and Self show up in action
- Consider how we can recognize and choose Self-led action (versus self-protective action)
- Discover ways to practice this optimal state of *being* in our everyday *doing* as a community
- Understand how to apply Self-led action in our approach to engaging and coaching students

The question of action may be what led you to pick up this book in the first place. Educators are constantly on the lookout for new ways to get better results from students and work more effectively with colleagues and parents. In these cases, we're looking for a practical, productive shift in action. Sometimes we find something that works; other times, it just seems to add more busyness and can overwhelm us. Let's apply our understanding of Self and parts as we consider a different approach to action.

"As educators, we are doers, and we want solutions: actions that will help us and ultimately our students. We must first learn ourselves so that we can teach others. Once we have shifted our actions and way of being, our students feel it. We can then operate together from a more optimal state of being—Self-leadership—which allows us to be truly present and do our very best. With commitment, resources, and intention, a culture can grow that benefits all members of the community."

—**Kathryn Serino,** former public school superintendent, Connecticut

Understanding Parts and Self in Action

The flow of our school day is a string of individual and collective actions and thus, a play of parts within and between us. In every moment of action, there is a part of us driving our behavior, operating from its unique set of values and fulfilling its role of trying to get our needs met. Depending on which parts lead the way, we will interact and react very differently to the situations we face.

As an example, I'll offer my observations of my own parts that have recently been at play—see if any of this sounds familiar to you. Over the past few months, as I've been developing and delivering a new workshop, I have noticed two teams of parts inside me: There are the parts of me concerned with getting the project and event done. I've come to recognize these parts as my production team. They are concerned with *producing* results, *perfecting* the outcome, *performing* so I impress others, and ultimately *proving* my worth. This team of protective manager parts is very busy and often exhausted. Then there are the parts with a seemingly opposite agenda. They serve as the antidote to the intensity of the production team, their efforts focusing on reassuring and comforting me. Some of these parts are more concerned with *pleasure*, encouraging me to sleep in, bake a batch of cookies, scroll social media, or go out for coffee with friends. Meanwhile, some of these parts are focused on *procrastination*; under the guise of "responsibility," these parts justify all the other work I need to prioritize before facing the complexity of finishing a big project. This team of protective firefighter parts has also worked hard to keep a sense of inner overwhelm at bay.

These parts have not only impacted my experience as I work alone but also influenced the work of my team. Whenever my team and I work together, my parts come with me. There are times when my "production team" parts show up at our meetings with some intensity. Thankfully, my team members have skillfully spoken for their parts, letting me know when I've caused some of their parts to feel overwhelmed and frustrated. It is so helpful and generous of them to point out the ways I affect our collective well-being and effectiveness. Being offered a glimpse of my blind spots has supported me in getting to know my parts that arise around work projects. As I've journaled, followed U-BAC, and invited these parts to be with me, I have appreciated the importance of their roles and explored how they can dial down so I can operate with balance and be more deliberate in when and how I embody each part. This U-BAC practice has also helped me honor who I am, what I am capable of, what I know, and what I have experienced that gives me ease and confidence to do my work. As I access this remembrance, I've also learned to recognize a palpable shift in my body as I rest into feeling more Self-led. Rather than tensing my body, leaning forward, and breathing shallow (which happens when I'm blended with my productive parts), I notice I can sit up tall with a sense of dignity, breathe in a relaxed manner, and embody my capacity to serve with strength and presence.

Often what blocks us from taking Self-led action is a polarization between protective parts. The drive of managers trying to be good and get stuff done comes into conflict with the instincts of firefighters to feel good and comfort us. A part of you wants to clean and organize your house, but another part wants to sit and enjoy a game of checkers with your child. A student might promise they are committed to engaging and doing their best work, but soon you see them distracted and goofing around . . . again. This battle in our heads is often how we undermine our own best intentions. However, when we see the two sides of the polarization, we can appreciate the positive intent of both sides. If we can mediate internally, our parts can often dial down and work with us to find a balanced approach. Above all, this practice of noticing parts gives us breathing space from being unconsciously driven by any one part. As a result, we start to access choice. This is the zone where Self-led action flows.

Pause and Reflect

- Consider a moment when you saw a student or colleague exhibit behavior you found difficult:
  - What happens if you try to imagine the part that was driving their action?
  - How might this part have been trying to protect them?
  - How were you impacted by this part of them?
- Now consider a moment in your work when you felt stuck or off your game:
  - Can you identify any part or parts of you that were driving?
  - How were these parts trying to help or protect you?

The Experience of Self-Led Action

Self-led action is not a stagnant state of accomplishment. It is an active practice, one that we nourish by continually building *awareness* of our parts. Fueled by our value for *understanding* others, Self-led action is discovered moment to moment as we purposefully engage with connection to Self and parts, one task at a time. The accumulation of these moments builds our ability to be more and more Self-led, resulting in a higher degree of purposeful, beneficial, and productive activity. We will naturally be less me-focused and more us-focused, considering the collective impact of our actions. This empowers us to act from our deepest wisdom and creativity.

While our external context and choice of action is personal, there are common characteristics to the internal experience of Self-led action. There is often a palpable physical shift into a calmer state, a sense of openness and heightened awareness, and a bit of breathing space from our more reactive protective parts. In this state, we get up to date with who we are: *Oh right, I am not a scared kid or an overwhelmed teenager. I am an adult with training for this job, capacity to figure things out, resources to access, people who can help me, the power to make choices, and a wish to give my best to support others. I am safe, I am okay, I am able.*

We might also remember some of our unique traits, gifts, or callings: *I am gifted as a teacher and able to build connections with students and break down tough ideas. I am uniquely positioned to build community and inspire hope. I've got this!* This remembrance positions us to rest into Self and hear our more self-protective parts without putting them in charge of our response strategy.

From this remembrance, we can also clarify our intention: *What is my purpose here? What is my goal and how does it serve my/our larger vision?* Our intentions lift us out of our limited stories about ourselves and the situation and instead place our action in a meaningful context. When we are Self-led and guided by an intention, we are poised to engage from more Self-led parts and recognize what action will be of greatest service.

Pause and Reflect

- Think of a moment in your own experience of being Self-led in the midst of school:
  - What was happening inside you?
  - What was your inner space like—physical sensations, thoughts, feelings?
  - What parts of you were in the lead? (perhaps listening calmly)
  - What parts did you choose not to follow? (perhaps your instinct to react and correct)
- Now take yourself a little further back in time and consider what you did that set you up for this experience of Self-leadership:
  - What choices did you make?
  - What practices supported you?
  - What frame of mind impacted your approach?

Self-led action is also characterized by a balance of intentional effort and soft surrender—an ability to flow with the moment. For example, an educator plans to discuss a student's performance with their parent and then bring the student in to explore a new way forward, but the plans are disrupted. Maybe the parent couldn't make the meeting due to a work emergency or the student ended up being sick. With so much that is not in our control, acting from Self-leadership is never a single action but an ongoing practice of reflecting on and realigning our intention with what the situation calls for.

Self-Led Action as a Community Practice

Finally, Self-led action can be recognized by the big-picture outcome of taking us out of *me*-level living and supporting us to connect with others in considering the *us*. When acting from Self, we are instinctively guided by an inner compass attuned to the greater good.

This brings us to a tricky aspect of Self-led action: Who is to say what action is good? Is it all subjective? Or can we collectively determine how we want to be together? It is essential to respect that characteristics and values vary in each community and culture. It is also fascinating how much we have in common, such as what we respect or how we aspire to be a good person. This often aligns with how we show up when we are Self-led.

Interestingly, this collective determination already happens in many school communities; we articulate common values that align with the best we know we are capable of. This expression of values informs our shared vision and individual activity. The words commonly seen on school emblems, banners over entrances, or posters in the front of classrooms, such as integrity, loyalty, steadfastness, respect, responsibility, discipline, caring, generosity, empathy, and tolerance, designate a set of values that the school community respects, rewards, and aspires to embody together. We can proactively study and explore these values as a community, use them to check our daily choices and procedures, and celebrate when they show up in our classrooms, meetings, and community functions. They can be used as tools to assist in decision-making, guide the quality of engagement, and support reflection on the impact of our actions when things go "wrong." In short, these values offer a shared language to define how we recognize Self-led action.

Recognizing Qualities of Self-Led Action

There are numerous ways to recognize and cultivate access to Self while taking action. In addition to the values generated by a community, we can utilize the 8 Cs as powerful markers of Self-led action. A teacher recently shared an example of this with me. She received some challenging feedback from colleagues that made her doubt herself and how she had been teaching and coaching students for years. To combat her feelings, she was calling people to get reassurance and then going to the kitchen to find the perfect, comforting snack. In the midst of this, as her parts were spinning, her eyes caught sight of a card she had posted at her desk of the 8 Cs. As she glanced over the spectrum of qualities, she recognized that she felt almost no access to Self in that moment. This recognition helped her unhook from the drama. She could see her parts and hear their voices, but she was no longer submerged in their narrative. Compassion arose for her parts, and she started to see how this response pattern in her was not so much about this piece of feedback but an old story in her that went back to how her mother criticized her as a child. Now she had greater freedom to be in the moment and consider how she wanted to act.

In addition to the 8 Cs, there are six additional qualities of Self that emerge in interactions and action. We refer to them as the 6 Ps:

- Purpose
- Presence
- Perspective
- Persistence
- Playfulness
- Patience

NOTE: Five of these qualities are identified in the IFS model as significant for healthy relationships; we have added *purpose* to the list, given its importance in coaching children in their exploration of action.

You can review these qualities before taking action to consider if your action will be relatively Self-led. You can also call on these qualities in the moment to create a pathway back to Self when you get knocked off course. Finally, you can use these qualities after you've taken action to reflect on how you showed up and the results of your actions.

Let's further explore how each of the 6 Ps serve as a valuable lens for action and inspire self-reflection as we navigate the realm of action.

The 6 Ps for Self-Led Action

PURPOSE

When we approach action with a clarity of purpose, we hold our vision in mind and set meaningful intentions. We consider the implications that ripple from our actions, not just to those around us, but also to our world as a whole and to future generations. We feel part of something greater than ourselves—acting with purpose is about *us*, not about *me*.

For example, a student is in the school counselor's office, called in for a pattern of littering in the school hallways. The student explains they don't feel cared for by teachers, so they aren't inspired to show care back. When asked what they do care about, the student lights up about caring for local wildlife and talks about a project they are on to prevent development on the public open space near their house. Validating the student's enthusiasm, a conversation unfolded to explore what was needed for this same sense of purpose to manifest at school.

PRESENCE

In acting from presence, we remember the innate value of who we already are and intentionally show up ready to be of service to the moment, rather than hijacked by parts with stories about the past or future. This quality of being puts others at ease; their parts feel safe and seen. Having presence is intertwined with being present in the moment, focused on what we are doing, and attuned to the evolving circumstances and what needs our attention.

For example, the superintendent and curriculum specialist from central office notify a teacher of a walk-through assessment of the school the next day. Many parts of the teacher are activated wondering how she might be judged and how she needs to prepare and perform to please them. Then she pauses and remembers her 25 years of teaching and connects with her confidence to simply show up and be herself, present in the moment.

PERSPECTIVE

Acting from perspective serves as an antidote to parts that want to be perfect and get it right. Rather than just seeing the options of good and bad or right and wrong, we perceive myriad viewpoints, experiences, and needs, and we even intentionally invite them in for consideration.

For example, a typically straight-A student comes after school for support with a big project that is due the next day. They haven't worked as much on it as they had planned, and thus, they are in tears. Their teacher listens and acknowledges their positive intent to make it perfect, then wonders if there are other ways to complete the project. This frees the student to brainstorm a new plan of action.

PERSISTENCE

Persistence supports the appreciation that our greatest discoveries often come from working through mistakes and challenges. While short-term gratification can derail our focused progress, persistence fuels the development of knowledge, skill, and self-esteem.

For example, halfway through the semester, a student with slipping grades acknowledges that it's hard to choose doing math homework after school when all their friends are online playing video games. The student's mom offers an invitation to persist, painting a picture of how they might feel if they fulfill their goals. The student remembers and reengages in steadfast effort while also making some time for fun with friends.

PLAYFULNESS

From the earliest moments of life, playfulness is at the heart of Self-led action. While playfulness often gets written off the list of to-dos because it's not seen as productive, it is actually through play that learning is tested and integrated and our innate wisdom and most creative solutions can shine forth.

For example, on a bleak winter afternoon, a teacher trying to push through the curriculum is discouraged by her students' lack of engagement. Listening to the pulse of the moment, the teacher lets go of her planned agenda and invites the students to stand in a circle to act out the characters from their book.

PATIENCE

We are often taken out of Self by our many parts that are driven by our notions of time—measuring our value based on how much we get done in a certain block of time. When we act with patience, we embrace what we can do with the time we have, planning realistically and finding a balance in our activities. Patience empowers us to choose the optimal path rather than the most expedient or convenient. Patience brings us into harmony with the present moment; we sink into the rhythm of what is happening and trust the process unfolding in the moment.

For example, a school principal recognized that she always felt rushed yet still believed she wasn't getting enough done. Inspired at an educators' retreat, she decided to experiment with taking the time needed to do each task well and adding in a pause between activities, like making a cup of tea or walking down the hall. She acknowledged she gets just as much done but feels more at ease and her work is better quality.

Proactively Cultivating Self-Led Action

The practice of Self-led action can be developed by purposefully using the 6 Ps to inspire and guide our actions through the day. That said, acting from Self does not mean living from a constant state of 8 Cs and 6 Ps all the time. It is much more about remembrance and practice. It means showing up to serve and love others *as we are in that moment*, imperfect but present. In fact, this is one of the greatest gifts we can offer students: the opportunity to grow alongside adults who embrace their wholeness, their parts, and their mistakes as a part of the great learning adventure of life.

Coaching Self-Led Action in Students

There is no doubt that learning through action is impactful and worthwhile. Many of our schools already rely on the power of action for teaching social skills and promoting community values. We develop classroom agreements to embody behavioral standards, such as respect, kindness, generosity, integrity, dedication. We practice and teach students decision-making skills, problem-solving, conflict resolution, and criteria for making good choices. We engage in fundraisers and community service. Our intention is that through these real-life daily experiences, students will learn emotional intelligence and interpersonal skills, and demonstrate wisdom and kindness in their actions.

Given the effort we make to teach by example, it can be puzzling when we see that our students haven't integrated the lesson. They often struggle to recognize and choose what we would consider Self-led action. Sometimes students just passively follow along without connecting the dots between the action and the underlying values it reflects, or worse, feel told what to do (e.g., "Be responsible" or "Play nice") rather than experiencing intrinsic motivation to be a good community member. It's extra baffling when we see apparently mindless, selfish, or harmful behavior, such as graffiti on the school property, rude manners, bullying on text threads, and damage to property. So many students seem to lack an inner compass, an ability to discern what behavior is beneficial for themselves and others. Rather than being concerned with their impact on others, they are preoccupied with external messages to embrace *me*-focused living, concerned with how they look, what they can get, and if they are liked. This is symptomatic of our societal crisis of identity and purpose, a loss of focus on choosing action for the greater good.

Self-led action runs counter to mainstream culture and thus requires great confidence and courage on the part of educators. Our students need our support, clarity, and guidance to understand and cultivate Self-led action. But while we hold the vision for noble, ethical action they could take to support their authentic well-being, students are often repelled by our managerial "be good" parts and respond with protective parts of their own. How do we coach the best in our students without energizing the opposite? How do we support them to notice the physical, emotional, and mental signals when they are acting in a Self-led state? How do we help them connect with their inner motivation to serve the greater good and not just their short-term interests?

The answer is through coaching. Engagement in action is a constant in the course of a school day, yielding hundreds of moments for an educator to coach a student through action. Each unique moment requires a unique response best discovered by accessing the state of Self together. Our job is to help students discriminate what parts are needed in any given situation. Is now a time to persist on their purpose to practice hockey even if they miss the movie with friends? Or is now the time to be playful, drop the agenda, and go have fun?

Being effective coaches requires us to ask the same questions of our parts. When and where do students need us to be *disciplined* and hold and guide them? When do they need us to let go and trust and be *accepting*? Let's consider these two sides by placing them on a scale.

On one side of the scale is discipline. At its best, discipline functions like the banks of a river, containing and channeling the water's energy to successfully move toward its destination. It supports us in building healthy habits and the capacity to be effective. Through our guidance, it is hoped that students internalize a healthy sense of self-discipline so they can realize their goals and potential.

As we know well, discipline can also be taken to an extreme when it is implemented by "power over" parts in adults. Instead of feeling guided, children likely feel judged, not trusted and controlled, and may be robbed of their independent voice and motivation. This can produce shame in children, which, in turn, generates self-protective parts such as an inner critic or an inner task master. For this reason, discipline needs to be kept in balance by the other side of the scale: acceptance.

Acceptance means providing children freedom and space to venture out, explore their world, try new things, and discover what they are capable of. To support this natural, healthy process, we need to step back, trust them, and welcome them as they are. Instead of trying to control their actions, we acknowledge their effort, celebrate their unique gifts, and allow them to experiment with choices and leadership. Open-hearted acceptance puts a child at ease and gives them the confidence to share their voice and try new things. Acceptance nurtures Self-led parts, such as self-compassion, presence, and playfulness.

As with discipline, going too far in the direction of acceptance can be harmful. If we operate from parts of us that are too permissive or even unavailable, letting children freely navigate on their own, they may feel unprotected. When they don't feel guided, they can flounder, feel anxious, and develop more protective parts to manage and care for themselves.

Reflecting on this balance for ourselves—*Am I more the accepting type or the disciplined type?*—can help us recognize different parts of us that show up in relationships with young people. Different circumstances tend to make us swing from one end to the other. A scale, as seen in the following image, can be used as a tool for self-reflection and to assess what is needed. While there is a time for calm and compassion (more accepting), there are also times to be clear and confident (more disciplined). Finding balance isn't a stagnant state; rather, it involves a constantly dynamic inquiry and a moment-to-moment practice of Self-led action.

The Dynamic Balance of Guiding Young People

Acceptance

Ask: Is now a moment that needs me to be . . .

- Appreciative
- Acknowledging
- Flexible/able to compromise
- Accommodating
- Understanding
- Welcoming
- Unconditional
- Easeful
- Open-minded
- Encouraging
- Nurturing
- Trusting

What will benefit this interaction?

Purpose
Presence
Perspective
Persistence
Playfulness
Patience

Discipline

Ask: Is now a moment that needs me to be . . .

- Setting limits and boundaries
- Holding expectations
- Consistent
- Firm
- Following through
- Focused
- Purposeful
- Reflecting impact of actions
- Guiding
- Delaying gratification

Search and Experiment: PAUSE for Self-Led Action

Pause and Reflect

- What are some of the steps you take to choose intentional and beneficial action?
- What is your recipe to act purposefully and learn from your experiences?

Now that we've considered how we recognize Self-led action, we will consider practical skills for embodying it. Many of these skills reflect commonly known best practices for decision-making, problem-solving, and conflict resolution, but here we'll reexamine them with an eye for how we can enact Self-leadership and inspire Self-leadership in others.

In the PAUSE model, the *S* and *E* guide Self-led action. After we've *paused* to reconnect with Self, become *aware* of where we are coming from, and made the effort to *understand* each other, there is often a natural moment when our parts relax into the knowledge that we are okay, and we begin to wonder together: *What are our options? What are we going to do?* From here, action comes in two main steps:

1. **Search for solutions that serve:** Assess what needs attention, brainstorm possibilities, and choose a course of action
2. **Experiment:** Take purposeful action, accept changing dynamics, and reflect on the results

Let's break these down further in the next sections.

The *S* of PAUSE: Search for Solutions that Serve

When presented with a problem or challenge, our knee-jerk reaction is often to jump to a solution. We may have many parts wired up to fix, help, and resolve. We want to convene with others involved, perhaps with a sense of urgency, and figure out what we are going to do. With the *awareness* to befriend our parts and connect with the needs of others, we gain access to our core capacity to move intentionally into action. While sometimes the next action becomes immediately apparent, there are times we need to slow down and deliberately consider our choice in action. This deliberate approach is captured by the idea of *searching* for solutions, the S of the PAUSE model.

Searching creates an opening to perceive options, assess benefit and impact, and choose mindful action. In searching, we explore *us*-focused questions: What is needed now? What might be possible? What supports our purpose and will serve the situation? What is in our power? Before stepping into action, we consider the essential elements of searching for solutions:

- Remember our common purpose
- Recognize context and what needs attention
- Brainstorm possibilities for moving forward
- Choose a course of action, recognizing what is in our power and what will serve the situation

Remember Your Common Purpose or Goal

Searching for solutions begins with reconnecting to what calls us into this shared space: our unifying purpose. This moves individuals from being opposite each other (or even in conflict) to playing on the same team. Unblended from parts that are focused on being right or in control, we can acknowledge the complexity of the situation and the different needs and experiences of others as well. This practice of remembrance is a transformative shift in which we can access a truly different way of operating: genuinely collaborating with the collective well-being in mind.

Recognize Context and What Needs Attention

Before we brainstorm solutions, we need to identify what it is that needs attention. This might begin by returning to what caused us to *pause* in the first place. Sometimes it's a past event that requires attention: someone was hurt, harm was done, there was a misunderstanding, or an error was made. These situations require attention in the form of acknowledgment or restorative action. In other cases, what needs attention is something in the future, such as a presentation, a conversation with a supervisor, or a deliverable on a project. It may be that there is an ongoing situation, such as student who has emotional or behavioral issues or is struggling academically and needs support. In other instances, we need to direct attention toward our shared purpose. Identify the focus of your collective attention and what you are working to address.

Brainstorm Possibilities for Moving Forward

At times, it can be very hard to imagine a different possibility while inside a situation and its associated mindset. To pull yourself out of a limited or stuck perspective, you can try one of the following strategies:

- Scan to see what part of yourself you are operating from. Notice your perspective and story about the situation. See if that part can step back to let you entertain other points of view.
- Remember a time when things worked out. What made that possible?
- Picture yourself in your desired future and imagine what could work.
- Consider what you would tell a friend in this situation.

- Shift your physiology by pausing; take a few deeper breaths or get up to move around.
- Invite more or different people to brainstorm possibilities.

Rather than developing options and possibilities from our hardworking "figure it out" parts, we can approach our brainstorming process through experiencing the qualities of Self. For instance, a spirit of playfulness invites brainstorming that is creative and initially uncensored, while taking a pause opens the door to inspiration. Brainstorming from the state of Self helps us glimpse unimagined options that will serve and benefit our community. A situation that initially seemed limited or even unworkable can transform into an opportunity with multiple possibilities.

Choose a Course of Action

Once we've opened our imagination to multiple possibilities, our focus turns to deciding on a course of action. An overarching question in this step is *What is in my power?* In any given situation, there may be a lot that we wish we could change but can't. We can't force a family that has endured trauma to attend therapy. We can't immediately or single-handedly change state or federal laws that obstruct what we see as effective instruction. We can't get rid of a colleague whom we think is incompetent or annoying. Since focusing on what is not in our power can feed a sense of frustration and hopelessness, we must purposefully shift our attention to what is in our sphere of influence and what we will use as criteria for choosing a course of action.

Along with values and context, the 6 Ps can help us assess which action to take by determining what will allow us to lead from Self—that is, release the expectation or need to be perfect and find courage to try an action that is "good enough" for the situation in front of us:

- **Purpose:** What best reflects my/our vision and intention?
- **Presence:** How can I/we be present and respond to the needs of the moment?
- **Perspective:** Can I/we see multiple viewpoints and possibilities?
- **Persistence:** What choice reflects the spirit of discipline and steadfast effort?

- **Playfulness:** What allows for fun, creativity, and joy to flow?
- **Patience:** What is best at this time and place, accepting that things unfold in time?

In sorting through our options, we must acknowledge that we generally don't know the perfect choice or what the full impact will be. Often, all we can do is choose what appears best in the moment and experiment to see what happens. On the brink of action, we must continue to be *aware* of our parts, such as self-doubt ("I can't do this"), overwhelm ("It's too much"), or blame ("It's really their fault; they should fix this"). Acknowledge these parts and their concerns, then remind them that while you may not know exactly what will happen as a result of your action, you can handle this situation and will figure out what to do next.

This consciousness of your parts will directly benefit others, especially students who are with you for the ride. When they see you grapple with mixed feelings about moving into action and then befriend these parts of yourself, they see you find your strong, responsible, courageous core from which you have the power to take purposeful action. What a gift for young people to witness this!

The *E* of PAUSE: Experiment for Self-Led Action and Reflect on the Results

As mentioned earlier, any action, no matter how carefully chosen, will bring us into contact with a variety of factors that are out of our control. With this in mind, the *E* in the PAUSE model guides us to approach action like a scientist. Scientists know that on their journey to discovery, they will do many experiments that yield a variety of results, many of which may be called failures. In that same spirit, embarking on action means testing options with courage and curiosity, deliberately reflecting on the results and celebrating our discoveries along the way. This is the heart of learning.

The following are the essential elements of *experimenting* for Self-led action:

- Embody purposeful action
- Engage in self-reflection on your action
  - Acknowledge yourself
  - Be curious to learn

Embody Purposeful Action

Following through on our plan for action calls for being present as we attend to the situation unfolding in real time. The 6 Ps come to life as we practice enacting Self-leadership. We must keep perspective and persevere, adjusting to changing circumstances. We foster patience as things unfold, playfulness to create and engage, and purpose as we realize our intention, even amid factors outside of our control.

In addition, as we experiment with action, we can practice attuning to our bodies, noticing signals of Self and stress and making microshifts to reconnect to Self as needed. Perhaps we deepen our breath, stand tall, or slow down. In this way, we embody our intention for how we want to show up.

As we see our experiment play out, we may draw on many of the tools we've discussed thus far: *pausing* to reset and anchor into Self, becoming *aware* of where we are coming from, making time to *understand* the other person's perspective, *searching* for new solutions together, and *experimenting* again. In action, as with all other steps, Self-leadership is a moment-to-moment practice in the flow of daily life.

Engage in Self-Reflection on Action

How do we know if we are Self-led in our actions? There isn't any tool that can tell you in the moment of action if you are connected to Self or not—only you know from your inner experience. This is also why it is beneficial to set aside some time after you take action to reflect, notice the results, and join with others involved in your action to offer and receive feedback.

There are two aspects to reflection:

1. **Acknowledge yourself:** We're often so busy being self-critical that we bypass this powerful and important practice. Acknowledgment, whether alone or with others, empowers us to see goodness and benefit in our efforts. Our defenses can rest knowing we are safe and valuable. Acknowledgment rapidly shifts us into a greater experience of Self-leadership—confidence, courage, and curiosity. With these qualities on board, we are positioned to be curious about areas for growth, and wc arc also in a state to receive and express Self-led feedback.

2. **Be curious to learn:** Every experiment gives the scientist new information: what worked, what didn't, and what to try next time. Similarly, our process of taking action and reflecting afterward continually feeds us new information that helps us refine our next action. With repetition, this process carves new pathways in our brains; we develop more effective habits, traits, and skills. A spirit of curiosity creates healthy feedback systems that fuel inspiration, confidence, and motivation.

NOTE: Inviting feedback is always well-intentioned, but how many people are able to stay open to feedback without walling off their heart? For that matter, how many people can effectively deliver information so others can take it in and hear it? Whether we are self-assessing or giving feedback to others, a genuinely curious reflection entails being open to the perspective and information from our different parts. Even our more negative, judgmental parts often hold very valuable information; if these parts could dial back and communicate with 50 percent less intensity, what might we learn from them?

Tips for Guiding Self-Led Action for Young People

Learning relies on being curious about the whole of our experience, not just delighting in our successful actions but wondering about the surprises, snags, and even perceived failures. This recognition must inform the way we guide our students through the process of choosing and taking Self-led action, whether in an individual context or in a group, like a classroom.

Honor Core Worth and Call Forth Potential

Guiding children requires us to hold the complex whole of who they are—the parts that are manifesting challenging behavior along with the core Self that we see and remember. Rather than getting stuck with limiting labels (e.g., "the angry kid") or diagnoses (e.g., "she's ADHD"), we find moments to pause and be present with the child we are supporting. We reaffirm their inherent worth when we look beyond the present circumstances to see the unique qualities we appreciate in them and remind them what they are capable of: "I know the effort you put into school. I've seen such thoughtfulness in your actions. I admire your strength coming to school even on days that feel hard for you."

Give as Much Responsibility as They Can Handle

From the moment they are born, a child's job is to try new things and test boundaries so they can do more today than they did yesterday. Our job, as adults, is to discover how much freedom to allow and where to set the boundaries so they are safe and set up for success.

Sometimes we overestimate what students are capable of. For example, we might expect them to know how to regulate their emotions and engage respectfully during a conflict, when, in reality, they simply haven't built the skills yet. On the other hand, we sometimes underestimate what they can do. We may feel the need to prescribe each specific task and assignment to teenagers even though they are fully capable of independent self-motivated engagement and contribution. How do you know if you are giving too much or too little responsibility? Discuss this with the child—explore if they feel overly challenged or set up for success.

When engaging in action with students, let them run with as much responsibility as they can handle. Ask them questions to spark brainstorming: "What do you think might work here? What is in your power?" Be available as a resource to provide information and offer guidance as needed: "I think ____ in your idea could work. Can I offer one suggestion? How about . . ." Make space for them to shine and cultivate self-confidence. We can let students take the lead, knowing there is a time and place to be a resource, to step in with new skills and information that can help them discern and select Self-led action.

Engage Them in Decision-Making

Interpersonal neurobiologist Dr. Daniel Siegel (2011) acknowledges how every time we allow children to exercise their muscle of decision-making, it builds their prefrontal cortex—what he calls their "upstairs brain." As the prefrontal cortex strengthens, it further builds their capacity to self-regulate and engage productively.

Encouraging this development can be as simple as asking students how they would like things to be and what they think would work: "What should our agreements/social contract/norms be? What will help you show up as your best

Self? How should we handle things when there is a conflict? What do you suggest are fair expectations for how much time you spend on homework? What schedule would best support you in learning today?"

Engaging students in the decision-making process lets them know that their needs matter and makes them feel seen for their capacity to think and contribute. It also helps mitigate any surprise they might feel when you implement expectations and limits. You may even find (to your own surprise) that they welcome your parameters.

Proactively Share Healthy Expectations and Boundaries

While engaging children and considering their input is vital in guiding Self-led action, the adult must be the leader for the system, setting expectations and maintaining boundaries. However, as we've seen, this Self-led leadership is palpably different from what most students are used to. Far from being controlling or displaying power over students, Self-led leadership conveys confidence, clarity, and courage. Educators lead the system in Self-led action by proactively sharing a realistic vision for what is possible and setting expectations and boundaries that align with that vision. When these expectations and boundaries are shared and understood beforehand, it won't be as confusing or shocking to a student when you follow through with them.

Encourage Self-Reflection

Feedback, assessment, testing, and grading are all ways we communicate performance evaluation. Ideally, these tools are given and received in a Self-led manner so that students can genuinely discover their areas for growth. However, these tools very often elicit protective parts. Feeling threatened and judged, students try to ward off feeling bad with parts that exhibit defensiveness, self-criticism, competitiveness, perfectionism, blame, lying, refusal, arguing, and so on. While we don't have the power in our positions to change the school and state expectations for testing and assessment, we can acknowledge students' parts that come forward regarding tests and exams; furthermore, we can design other fruitful opportunities of self-acknowledgment, self-assessment, and self-reflection. At the end of the day, students want to know we love and respect them and that we will continue to protect and support them.

Conclusion

Self-led action is not a destination, but a continual practice of coming back to center and choosing the next best move. As we work to integrate this practice, we can use multiple lenses to assess and guide our actions, including:

- School values (e.g., integrity, respect, discipline)
- The 8 Cs: calm, compassion, courage, curiosity, confidence, clarity, creativity, and connection
- The 6 Ps: purpose, presence, perspective, persistence, playfulness, and patience
- The balance scale: acceptance versus discipline
- Questions for Self-led action:
  - What needs my/our attention?
  - How does this support my/our purpose?
  - What are my/our options and possibilities?
  - What is in my/our power? What will be of service?

These lenses support us to prepare for Self-led action, engage effectively, and reflect on our learning. As we coach students in Self-led action, we nurture a productive and vibrant learning process and culture. Through the practice of Self-led action, we are empowered to realize our potential individually and collectively.

Stories from the Field

Starting with Ourselves, We Can Bring Hope to Our Students

Dr. Melissa Zych is a music teacher at Charter Oak International Academy, an international baccalaureate and Title I charter school in Connecticut.

I'd spent the last 24 years focused on teaching through a social-justice lens in a Title I school. Recently, I earned a doctorate in educational leadership and felt a growing curiosity in how my work could benefit a larger number of students and teachers. During this same period, I read professional journals and attended many professional development workshops that grappled with the issues of trauma, student dysregulation, and teacher burnout. The more I read and reflected on these issues, the more I realized that the way we were teaching and managing behaviors for the past 20 years needed to change. When I heard about this workshop for educators to learn about Self-leadership, I felt like it was worth a try to see if it could help our students and teachers. I had no idea how much it would not only transform my teaching, but profoundly shift my understanding and experience of myself.

My first interaction with parts language at school came when I was called to a nearby classroom to help. There was a student who was underneath a table and refused to come out. When I arrived, I opened the door and quietly signaled for him to come into the hallway. He came with me right away, thank goodness! At first, I reacted habitually, telling him that he needed to follow directions. Then I remembered what I was learning. I paused for a moment and took a deep breath. I told him that it looked like a part of him was very upset (he was crying and breathing hard) and wondered if he could tell me what was going on. He explained that he was mad because the substitute teacher was not following the routine of the class, and he felt like things were out of control. I told him that I realized how hard it can be to have someone different and new that didn't know the way things usually go. "It can be so frustrating," I said.

After this acknowledgment of the part that felt mad, I asked him if he could identify other parts of him. He told me about his calm part. I asked him if he thought that this part could take over for him. "Like, maybe, your frustrated and upset parts could sit down and chill out with a popsicle for a while, and then you could check in with them later." He agreed that this calm part would probably be a better fit for the work he needed to complete. Keep in mind that I never talked to this student about parts prior to this interaction. It was an incredibly positive first experience that I was able to build and reflect on.

My biggest takeaway on this PAUSE journey has been that if I want my kids to be more Self-led, then I must learn to lead from my best Self. It was uncomfortable, but I jumped in. This is not a formula, a list, or a quick-fix solution. It is deep. IFS has enabled me to get to know myself, understand why and under what circumstances certain parts come up, how to unblend, and how to get back to my best Self. I am more able to view my parts with curiosity and compassion.

The more I watch the magic of IFS unfolding in my life and my school, the more I appreciate the unique and powerful keys it gives us to address our core challenges and fundamental needs as educators. It offers healing for trauma, calm for dysregulated students, renewal for stressed educators, and a vision of hope that our schools can truly be joyful places for our next generation of leaders.

Invitations to Practice

CONTEMPLATE: *Cultivating Gratitude and Acknowledgment*

In this exercise, you will picture taking a walk through your daily life, especially at school, to notice what you are grateful for, to acknowledge what is working, and to be thankful for the abundance of what is. Take yourself on a mental journey of your school. Be on the lookout for what you are grateful for. Perhaps you notice a familiar tree, soft sunlight, a student's beautiful artwork, or all the resources you *do* have in your school. Perhaps you see the signs of Self in others—you see someone completing a mundane daily task and appreciate the effort, or you notice two friends laughing—the building blocks of human connection. Inside, make note and express gratitude for these gifts. Gradually you can also shift to yourself. You might reflect on your recent actions. What efforts have you made? How have you tried your best? How about being grateful to yourself just for waking up, showing up, and being here with your unique perspectives and gifts? Thank yourself. As you practice acknowledgment and connect to feeling grateful, notice the inner sensation. What happens inside you? Breathe into this space. This is Self.

WRITE: *Reflect on Parts that Drive Action*

List three parts of you that commonly drive your actions as an educator or caregiver.

____

____

____

Now pick one of these parts and consider the following questions:

In what ways does this part reflect qualities of Self and act in Self-led ways?

____

____

____

____

____

Does this part of you tend to be more accepting or more disciplined?

____

____

____

____

____

What is this part's positive intent, and how does it help students?

___

___

___

___

___

When this part is disproportional, a bit extreme, or cranked from a 5 up to a 10, what does this look like? What is the effect on students? What message do they get? What is their takeaway?

___

___

___

___

___

If this part could dial down or step back, how would you prefer to be in these situations?

___

___

___

___

___

WALK: *See the Big Picture*

As you walk, focus on the big picture. Focus on what's farthest from you, such as the horizon line or even a long open stretch down a street. Take in the whole of the space around you. Notice the effect in your body and mind as you practice this shift.

ACT: *Find Your Moments of Self-Led Action*

As you move through your day, make note of the moments you feel like you are acting from Self. What are the signs of Self-led action in your experience? Do you feel on your game, in the flow, or connected, clear, and courageous? What supports you to show up this way amid the myriad challenges and demands you juggle?

CHAPTER 5

The PAUSE for Self-Leadership Model

Pause and Reflect

- What are your best practices to effectively coach students through strong emotions, problems, or conflict?
- What have you explored through this book that aligns with what you already do intuitively on your best days?

PAUSE as a Process

To this point, we have delved into the core concepts and skills embedded in each element of the PAUSE for Self-Leadership™ model. In this chapter, we will look at how we operationalize these core concepts and skills by following PAUSE as a holistic process to guide everyday interactions. The more we study these concepts, the more they become the lens through which we see, understand, and respond in our everyday experience. Repeated practice of the five elements of PAUSE makes them easy to access when we need them most. The more we build our fluency with them, the more empowered we are to draw on the steps as they apply in each unique encounter. Rather turning into rigid protocols, the PAUSE process provides a flexible framework for responding to the dynamics of school from Self-leadership.

As we review the steps of the PAUSE model, imagine how you would apply them in a challenging moment, especially when parts are activated or effective action is called for.

P Is for Pause: What Is Happening Around and Inside Me? Am I in Self?

Very often, our primary issue is that we are running on autopilot, unaware of our inner state and what part of us is driving the show. Then, when we encounter a choice, a transition, or a stressor, we often proceed doing what we always have done: saying what's on our mind and seeing the problem as something outside of ourselves, jumping into action to fix. For this reason, when faced with a stressor or challenge, whether external or internal, the first and most essential step is literally to *pause*. Whether by ourselves or together with others, we step back, get perspective on what is happening, and take a breath.

As we pause, we also scan our inner experience and ask, *Am I connected to my authentic Self right now?* The key is to connect with a critical mass of Self before moving forward. Sometimes we need to do a brief self-reflection practice: watching our breath, feeling our feet on the ground, or scanning our body for signs of stress. If our buttons are really pushed, we may need to give ourselves a quiet moment, get up to move our body, or shift temporarily to a different task. Depending on the circumstances, it can take 20–60 minutes for our body and mind to downshift out of the stress response. We can use the 8 Cs and 6 Ps as a guide to help us assess and regulate our state.

After allowing space and silence for as long as we need (and the situation allows), we can look at the circumstances and take stock of what is happening around us. Just naming the situation can help us anchor our attention and show up for what the moment needs. However, it is generally not very productive to push for a conversation or solution to a problem when one or more people are activated. For this we move on to the *A* and *U* of the PAUSE model.

A Is for Aware of Myself: Where Am I Coming From?

After pausing, the next step is to become *aware* of our parts and notice which ones are activated in this moment. Often, when we are with students, our instinct is to jump over ourselves to help them be self-aware. However, awareness should start with ourselves—as they say on airplanes, "Put on your own oxygen mask first before helping others." When we are triggered, it is critical that we make space to be aware of and unblend from our parts, lest they continue to drive our actions.

In this step, we take a moment to scan inside, notice our parts (manifesting as thoughts, feelings, or sensations), and ask them for a bit of breathing space. We check if there is anything essential inside ourselves that needs immediate attention or needs to be spoken for with others. Often, this moment of self-acknowledgment puts our inner system at ease and allows us to focus back on the people we are with.

With that said, it is highly valuable to circle back to these parts of ourselves when we have time, especially if the part was particularly strong. Coming back to our parts later to say, "How are you? Tell me more about why you came up today" builds trust with our inner system. This helps our parts become increasingly cooperative and less likely to hijack us in moments of stress. (To spend time with a part and get to know its needs better, follow U-BAC, as discussed in chapter 2.)

U Is for Understand Each Other: Where Is the Other Person Coming From?

Once you've *paused* and become *aware* of what parts are activated in you, the next step is to have a conversation with the other people involved so you can *understand* each other's perspectives and needs. Regardless of whether we are dealing with people who also know the PAUSE model and have taken a pause with us, or with people who are not familiar with these concepts and are highly activated, we can practice listening from Self and speaking for parts.

Generally, the best place to start is with Self-led listening. If we can be the Self in the system, we can help the other person feel heard, seen, and acknowledged. This is especially true with young people. We may need to allow time and space to hear their story and perspective and reflect our understanding to them. (U-BAC can be a framework to guide this deeper listening as discussed in chapter 3.) Even in moments when we don't have a lot of time, we can make brief comments to show we are paying attention and appreciating their perspective.

The other aspect of understanding one another is the awareness of the interaction of parts in a conversation and speaking *for* parts rather than *from* parts. Even while we are listening to another, we can start to send out signals to the parts we see in them. For example, we could acknowledge the part's positive intent and effort. When someone else is blended with a part, we can listen to them and understand they are blended with a part without ever calling it a *part* out loud. As we reflect back our understanding, there may come a moment where we gently introduce parts language, saying something like "Wow, I get that a part of you is really frustrated about this . . ." Even if the person has never formally learned about parts, this use of language validates their experience while also reflecting that we understand it is not the whole of who they are. As we see the other person settle down and reflect more qualities of Self, we can also discriminate if it's helpful for us to speak for our parts. We can convey our experience, perspective, and needs through parts language. And once again, U-BAC can provide a framework to support how we express our parts' positive intent and underlying needs.

Of course, every conversation is organic and occurs in unique circumstances. As you dance between listening from Self and speaking for parts, the parts involved generally deescalate, and the people involved experience more connection to the signs of Self, including being more connected to each other.

S Is for Search for Solutions: What Needs Attention? What Might Be Possible? What Is in Our Power?

Once we get to the point that we *understand* each other (and are not blended with our parts), we can more readily perceive the whole of the situation, as well as the multiple possibilities for moving forward. This is a powerful moment to remember our purpose, listen into the situation from an "us" level, and *search* for an action that would be good for all parties. Sometimes, the first essential step is to acknowledge what has happened in the past: a hurtful word said, an unconscious behavior demonstrated, or a harmful action taken. When we name this past event and own our part in it, we lay the groundwork for trust that enables both parties to consider what is needed to move forward. Our options for action can be contemplated through the lens of the 6 Ps—what can we do that would reflect purpose, presence, perspective, persistence, playfulness, and patience? More simply, we can ask, *What choice of action will most likely allow us to experience and lead from Self together?*

When we are coaching students in this stage, we must balance offering acceptance with providing discipline. On one hand, we want to let them take the lead in suggesting next steps and imagining what will work. This gives them a sense of agency and allows them to develop their competence and confidence. At the same time, we need to provide clear boundaries and guidance reflecting our intention for them. Children don't know what they don't know, and we have an essential role to offer appropriate guidance. While all voices are welcome as we brainstorm options and attempt to choose a course of action together, there are times when the adult in the situation will need to make the final call.

E Is for Experiment: What Shall We Try? What Are We Learning?

In nearly all fields of science, *experiments* are the space to put a hypothesis to the test, try something new, and reflect on the results. We can apply this same mindset. Having accessed our best Selves, connected as a team, and brainstormed solutions, we take action to see: to see what happens, to see how it feels, to see what works. Approached this way, life is an adventure of learning. We are not a failure when things don't go as we expect; rather, we are learners. In the spirit of experimentation, we can practice taking action in a purposeful way—being present and focused, trying our best.

As we take the Self-led action we've chosen, we can track our experience of it, noticing the signs of embodied Self-leadership, such as a physical sense of calm, a confident approach, or clarity of thinking. Then, after the action has been completed, we can reflect on its results. Our protective parts generally go straight to assessing what didn't work, criticizing and judging what wasn't good enough. For this reason, we consciously begin with acknowledgment: noting the effort, celebrating the accomplishment, and seeing the positive impact. Once protective parts are put at ease by our appreciation of their positive intent, all parties are in Self together and can explore feedback for the sake of learning and growth. No one is blamed, shamed, or considered bad. Everyone benefits from learning, growing, and exploring.

Pause and Reflect

- Review a summary of the PAUSE model in the following table. As you study it:
  - Acknowledge how the model makes sense to you or excites you
  - Be curious about any questions or concerns you might have

PAUSE for Self-Leadership™ Model (Extended Version)

Pause and notice your state of being and connection to yourself.	What is happening inside and out? Am I my best Self? • Pause when you notice or anticipate a reaction. • Step back, breathe, and physically regulate. • Connect with your core Self: Focus on the 8 Cs (calm, compassionate, courageous, curious, confident, clear, creative, connected). • Remember who you are and what you are capable of.

Be ***Aware*** of your inner response and underlying needs.	Where am I coming from?
	• Notice parts of you showing up as thoughts, feelings, and physical sensations.
	• For parts needing your attention, follow U-BAC. Connect to your part from the space of Self:
	  - Unblend to be with your part as it presents right now.
	  - Befriend your part to hear its message and positive intent in this moment.
	  - Attend to your part, acknowledging what it needs at this time.
	  - Consider the 4 As to recognize the part's underlying need: acceptance, appreciation, assurance, assistance.

Understand each other.	Where are others coming from? Listen *from* Self to understand each other; connect with their parts. • As it benefits, speak *for* the different parts of you (not *from* your parts). • Say, "A part of me thinks . . ." or "A part of me feels . . ." • Appreciate each other's experience as multiple parts guided by U-BAC (unblend) and name the parts at play. See the parts' positive intent (befriend) and their different perspectives and needs (attend). Nurture connection.
Search for solutions that will serve the situation.	What needs our attention? What might be possible? What is in our power? • Remember your vision and common purpose. • Identify what needs attention. • Brainstorm possibilities for what could work moving forward. • Choose a course of action that will serve all involved. • Use the 6 Ps to recognize signs of Self-led action: purpose, presence, perspective, persistence, playfulness, patience.

Experiment in action.	What shall we try? What are we learning? • Collaborate as you take purposeful action to benefit your community. • Afterward, set a time to reflect on the result and impact of your actions. • Acknowledge positive intent, effort, and accomplishment. • Be curious about "mistakes" and "failures," exploring opportunities for growth.

Proactive PAUSE Micropractices

To follow the PAUSE process in the moments when we need it, it's beneficial to continue to study and practice the skills embedded in each element of the model. Fortunately, school life offers myriad opportunities to proactively explore and consider the concepts and skills in the PAUSE model. Through continual engagement in micropractices, we build our capacity to fluently and skillfully recognize parts and connect to Self even in the most intense or demanding moments. Here are a few areas of practice to consider for your own development and your work with others:

- **The 8 Cs and the 6 Ps:**
  - Post these qualities of Self in a visible area.
  - Consider your internal signs when you are embodying each quality.
  - Pick a quality each day to practice and enact.
  - Articulate who you know you are when you are in Self. Write this down so you can return to this when you need to remember your capacity and worth.

- **Pathways to Self:**
  - Schedule micropractices to help you reconnect to Self during the day, such as deep breathing, gentle movement, or noticing what you are grateful for.
  - Identify what practices reconnect you with Self when you have a bit more time, such as reflecting, writing, talking to friends, or walking in nature.
  - When you feel off your game or not yourself, pause and check to see your level of access to these qualities of Self. Is there one you can take hold of?
- **Awareness of parts:**
  - Be a parts detector. List or map parts rising and subsiding in yourself throughout the day or in any given situation.
  - Consider parts that commonly arise in you and others. What might be their positive intent?
  - When a specific part comes up, follow U-BAC.
- **Understanding others:**
  - Practice *you* listening. Listen with curiosity and compassion with the purpose of understanding. Do so without an agenda to fix, judge, or advise.
  - Naturally integrate speaking *for* parts in your daily conversations.
  - Notice and discuss the signs of parts in others in your school and also in characters from books, history, or movies.
  - Speak for your parts with each other in community spaces, including classroom circles, staff meetings, and project committees.
  - Externally represent your parts to others in fun ways, such as figurines, paint swatches, emojis, or drawings.

- **Self-led action:**
  - Get clear on your individual purpose and intention for your work—your why.
  - Discuss your common purpose—what brings you together as a community and how you want to be together.
  - Use the PAUSE model and the 6 Ps to inform processes to reflect on action and impact.

Stories from the Field

Integrating Micropractices for Class Culture

Amy Schaefer is an art teacher at a suburban public middle school in Connecticut.

I only get students for 40 minutes at a time and people ask how I have the time to integrate PAUSE micropractices. I tell them I can't afford not to!

To begin, I always stand outside my door to welcome students into class. I ask them to line up so I have a brief moment as each student enters for us to check in. They either hold their thumbs up, middle, or down. In this simple practice, they take a brief moment to *pause* and be *aware* . . . and I have a signal to *understand* where they are at. We then start every class sitting in a circle. Sometimes I lead a practice to pause and be mindful of our state and connection to Self. I also might invite students to use color swatches or figurines to represent their parts and then speak for them with classmates. These practices, which can take just five minutes, create the learning container. Everyone and their parts feel seen and welcomed. With this, we are ready to engage in learning together!

As you can see, I have intentionally woven proactive practices into my classroom so my students learn all the elements of PAUSE. In this way, when I want to use shared language of parts and Self to connect and shift how we are interacting, my students are ready with the self-awareness and interpersonal skills they need.

Through sustained practice of the elements of the PAUSE model in our learning communities, we increase our ability to interact and engage from Self-leadership as adults and students. As reflected in the following image, we grow our collective capacity to unblend from our parts, connect "heart to heart," and embody the 8 Cs and 6 Ps as we take action together. Picture what this would look like if proactively practiced in your learning community!

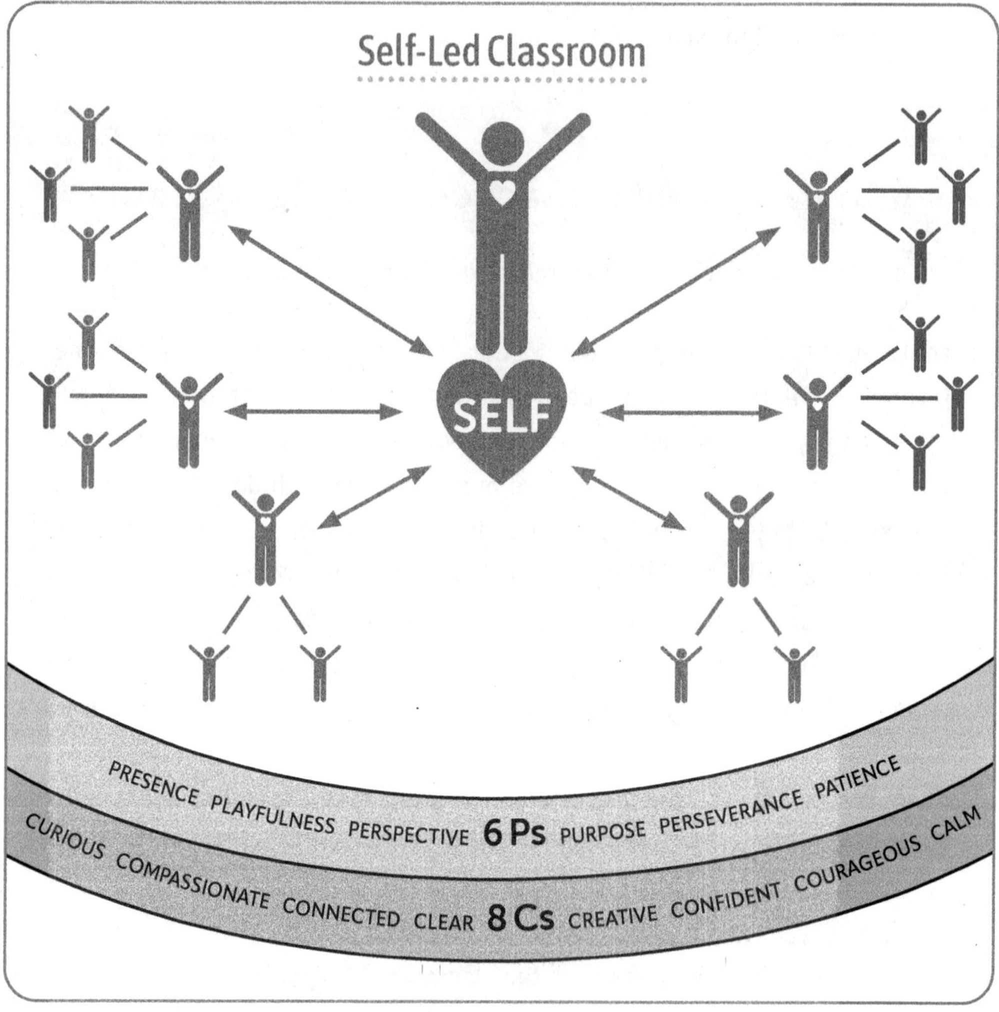

Through nurturing the qualities of Self and engaging in micropractices inspired by the PAUSE model, we can nurture a shared language, a Self-led learning environment, and a vibrant community culture.

A Cause to PAUSE: Using PAUSE to Guide Our Process

Once you become familiar with the elements of PAUSE, you can follow the model in many different ways. PAUSE can guide a collective process and provide shared language for two people or a group, such as a classroom community. Once fluent in PAUSE, certain steps can be followed and called on in the moment as needed. For example, picture that you are with a frustrated parent. With a *pause* for a quick inner scan, you recognize you are relatively Self-led, so you can move right to the practices of *understanding* to connect and attend to their needs. With time, the PAUSE model is less formal and linear and more of a dynamic and fluid process that continually informs your perception and response moment to moment. Finally, PAUSE is often experienced as a cycle. When we regroup at the end of the process to review the *experiment*, we often find that we are again traveling through the steps of the PAUSE model to reflect on where we are at and what is next.

To help you consider the practical and real application of this model in your school, we'll look at a few more *Stories from the Field* written by educators who have committed to daily self-reflection exercises guided by the steps of the PAUSE model.

PAUSE for Individual Reflection

You can use the PAUSE model to support your self-reflective process and to develop your own relationship with your inner system. You can also use it to prepare for a situation, during an interaction, or to guide your contemplation of what happened after the fact.

In all these instances, anticipating or perceiving another person's response often leads to a story about it: that it was extreme, unreasonable, uncalled for, or not fair. Stories like these are good indicators that our parts also are activated. The more we take time to *pause* in these situations, the more we increase our self-*awareness*, expand our *understanding* of others, and improve our effectiveness in navigating these types of situations going forward.

Stories from the Field

A Brief PAUSE in the Moment

Amy Schaefer is an art teacher in a suburban public middle school in Connecticut.

It was the end of the day; I was tired and a bit frustrated, but couldn't pinpoint why. I *paused* and gave myself a few moments just to sit and breathe, settling down and resting into the chair. I then noticed a part of me that felt agitated. *Aware* of this part, I asked what its story was. I was taken back to earlier in the day when a student showed up at class without a pencil. Unable to do the assignment, he'd ended up goofing around and distracting other students. This pushed my buttons, with a part of me feeling disrespected and annoyed. *Couldn't he just show up with a pencil?* Acknowledging this part, I started to feel more space inside and naturally turned to *understanding* my student. What might have been happening in his day? Where was he coming from? I recognized that from his perspective, this probably wasn't a big deal. He was just a 12-year-old kid who forgot his pencil—no harm intended! I was then able to *search* for solutions, imagining how I would handle this differently the next time it happened.

PAUSE with Students

As educators, we interact with students all day, helping them prepare for and navigate learning, changes, challenges, and stressors. In each of these interactions, we have the opportunity to follow the PAUSE model, further strengthening their capacity for emotional resourcefulness and relational skills. Some of these interactions take just a few minutes; in others, we may need to set aside more time for an in-depth engagement with students.

Stories from the Field

PAUSE to Shift from Activated to Available

Amy Schaefer is an art teacher in a suburban public middle school in Connecticut.

While practicing for a staff presentation one afternoon (about which I was nervous), a student barged in through the closed door without knocking. My initial reaction was to yell, "Lily, that was rude not to knock. Please leave." Instead, I felt the shift into Self-leadership: I *paused*, curious and compassionate about my parts that were being activated in me. I became *aware* that my annoyance had to do with my nervousness, not her actions. So, instead of yelling, I inquired why she was here after school and learned she had an interview to try out for a special academic program that afternoon, and she was extremely nervous! Speechless, I realized how my part would have gotten in the way of our connection and unintentionally stopped me from being *understanding*. Because I followed PAUSE, I was able to help her find her calm and feel ready. And in this case, that state of being was the only *solution* she needed.

PAUSE with Adults

While our instinct as educators is to consider how we can apply our learning in our work with students, it is also important to consider how we can practice the PAUSE model in our adult relationships. As you've probably experienced, the dynamics between adults often create the greatest stress and frustration. Teachers may feel that their administrator doesn't know their reality or appreciate their work, while principals may feel teachers don't appreciate the complexity of running a school or the logical reason behind difficult choices they make. Teachers may be frustrated with parents for not responding to emails or helping with homework, while parents may feel misunderstood and judged for their children's behavior, even though the parents are sincerely trying their best at home.

These disconnects between adults in our school communities create tension, inefficiency, and sometimes disengagement. And while we assume these dynamics are kept safely behind closed doors, students experience the effect of these interactions. For example, if teachers feel muzzled, unacknowledged, or talked down to, this feeling of unease will likely leak into their interactions with students. Conversely, if a principal practices the PAUSE model while engaging a teacher, the teacher will experience the principal's curiosity, compassion, and clarity and carry a feeling of goodness into their work with students. The composite of these daily interactions between adults channels directly into the heart of school climate.

Stories from the Field

Colleagues Follow PAUSE to Prep for Intervention

Steve Fitzgerald is a student affairs coordinator at a suburban public middle school in Connecticut.

Amy [Schaefer] called me to share an incident that had just happened in her class. A student had used derogatory language with a classmate, which led to a yelling match. Amy had managed to pull the students together, deescalate the situation, and stabilize things—thanks to the relationship she had with them—but the situation clearly needed more attention.

In my role as coordinator of student services, I invited Amy to come debrief the situation. My experience of this conversation was so remarkable because we both have training in the PAUSE approach. To start, we both *paused*, exhaled, and spoke for our parts. We were even a bit surprised as we became *aware* of how much we were impacted by the incident, the words said, and how intense it got so quickly. As we offered each other *understanding* and our inner systems calmed, we naturally turned to discussing the students and wondering about what had really happened. Together, we remembered more of the backstory of the student who said the hurtful statement. While we wouldn't ever endorse such behavior, we also were able to get in touch with the pain this student was living with daily. In brief interactions with his family, we'd gathered they had a high level of stress due to a parent losing a job and a family member with illness, and this pain was sadly getting directed at other students in angry outbursts. Amy and I could imagine a part of the student that was hurting (an exile) that was covered by a protective part that lashed out at classmates. This recognition generated a deep feeling of compassion for the student: true *understanding*.

As Amy and I came to this sense of connection with the student who had caused harm, we were able to approach planning for a genuinely restorative conversation with him and the student he'd spoken to. We were ready to hold a space that could be structured and safe while compassionately welcoming all parts.

Following the meeting with the students, we remarked at how extraordinary it was. The boy who'd caused harm came in guarded and on the defensive: protective parts on top. As we were in Self and facilitated from that space, both boys connected with us, and amazingly, by the end, with each other. Together, as we spoke for our parts, we were clear in conveying that boundaries were crossed (certain behaviors were not acceptable), but that we were confident in the boys' innate capacity to be responsible and curious about what kind of repair would mend the harm done. By the end, the boy who caused the harm voluntarily said, "Billy, I am truly sorry. That was mean . . . not cool . . . not my best. It won't happen again." He knew the *solution* that was called for; he had it inside him. Working from Self-leadership together, Amy and I operated as an intuitive and fluid team, attuning to the needs of the moment and capable of improvising because of our practice in using PAUSE.

PAUSE with Groups

As we work with groups of people, such as students in a classroom or faculty in a staff meeting, we can hold the PAUSE model as a process to guide our debriefing, planning, facilitation, and teaching. PAUSE can be used as a practical framework to structure a discussion on a sensitive or important topics (e.g., natural disaster, death of community member, sensitive academic topics) or to support collaborative team engagement (e.g., group projects, change management). Although our instinct in a group is to get down to business or dive into the matter at hand (the "S" and "E" of the PAUSE model), we inevitably show up with our unique perspectives, feelings, needs, and contributions. PAUSE facilitates a group of people to *pause* and be self-*aware*, to notice their experience and what they want to share. The *understanding* space ensures all viewpoints are welcomed and considered. Then *searching* for solutions supports collective brainstorming related to what is needed and what is possible before determining action for *experimentation*.

Stories from the Field

PAUSE for Whole-Class Practice and Response

Amy Schaefer is an art teacher in a suburban public middle school in Connecticut.

During class one day, I lost my cool because students were being unsafe in the classroom, not listening to directions, and being disrespectful. I yelled and was hijacked by my frustrations, and I immediately noticed one student's body language changed. His facial expression became tight, and when I asked him what was going on, he got angry and raised his voice at me. I gave him space to calm down, as I also needed some space to unblend. Though we both took our time, I was not letting the student get away with his actions; he knew this situation was going to be addressed the next day, as he was well aware of my classroom norms.

That night, I worked through my PAUSE practice. The next day in class, we formed a circle and followed PAUSE to guide our process. I told them part of me was angry because of the disrespect. Part of me was also scared because they were being unsafe, and another part was disappointed in myself because I yelled at them. I told my students I was grateful for the community we have built and want to give them a chance to speak for their parts.

When the student that was upset the day before had his chance to speak, I asked what parts of him were triggered. He said there was a side of him that thought it was funny. But a part of him was really angry that I had yelled at the whole class when he was not involved in any of the behaviors.

I reflected back, "It sounds like part of you was annoyed that you were yelled at?"

Agreeing, he went on to explain that he gets yelled at all the time at home and reacts by yelling back, so the same part popped up in him at school. He went on to share that I had never yelled before like that and it really bothered him. It was clear he trusted and expected me to be different from his family. It was amazing he was able to let me know how he felt!

Through the PAUSE practices implemented in a restorative circle, we were able to speak for our parts and have a calm and curious conversation as a whole class. I made sure to tell the class I was grateful for all of the parts expressed during the circle. All in all, the circle was no more than 10 minutes. Before learning the

PAUSE model, I probably would have stayed frustrated with the class and brushed it all under the carpet, having it happen again or having to get administration involved. Building community in my classroom with PAUSE helps all of us through the tough patches so we work to deescalate even the hardest situations.

Conclusion

The PAUSE model integrates the core concepts and skills for Self-leadership into a "hip-pocket" tool that you can apply when navigating your many interactions and situations, both big and small throughout the day. Following PAUSE has many benefits:

- Supports us as adults to be self-reflective and conscious as we respond to challenges
- Proactively builds our capacity for healthy, everyday relationships
- Allows us to respond in a confident, beneficial way when a student is activated or struggling, helping them regulate and reengage productively
- Supports us to be collaborative with fellow adults, addressing problems ranging from small to big and local to global

This model is not asking you to take on, know, or intervene more than you already do. Rather, it offers a fresh awareness and clear process to engage in the roles and relationships you already have every day. Imagine the ease this can provide if you continue to practice and integrate it yourself as a framework and reflective tool. What relief, clarity, or efficiency might it afford? With the PAUSE model, you can integrate Self-leadership as an authentic, dynamic way of *being* and *doing* in your daily life.

Invitations to Practice

WRITE: *Reflect on the Why Behind PAUSE*

Review the brief version of the PAUSE model in the table on the following page. Consider the underlying logic of the model. It is designed to make explicit best practices many of us follow intuitively when we are leading from Self. Ideally, you discover how the model resonates and makes sense for you, so you can integrate it fluidly and intuitively in the moment. To do this, consider the rationale of the steps and how they build on each other. You can ask yourself:

Why does it make sense to *search* for solutions that serve before *experimenting* with Self-led action?

____

____

____

Why is it valuable to *understand* each other before we try *searching* for solutions?

____

____

____

Why is it helpful to be self-*aware* before trying to *understand* others?

____

____

____

Why might we need to *pause* and check our connection to Self before we can be self-*aware*?

____

____

____

The PAUSE for Self-Leadership™ Model

Pause: What is happening outside and inside?
Step back, breathe, and connect to Self.

Aware of myself: Where am I coming from?
Notice my parts: thoughts, feelings, perspectives, and needs.

Understand each other: Where are others coming from?
Listen from Self and speak for parts.

Search for solutions: What might be possible?
Brainstorm what is for the good of all and identify what is in our power.

Experiment: What can we try?
Act purposefully, acknowledge accomplishments, and be curious to learn.

ACT: *Find the Moments to PAUSE*

As you move through your day, make note of the moments when it would benefit you to practice the PAUSE model either before, during, or after a situation. Keep a list of situations you can reflect on later following PAUSE. (You can then use these situations in the *PAUSE Process* practice in this chapter.)

VISUALIZE: *Picture the Impact of PAUSE*

Identify an interaction with a student or colleague that you want to understand better. Bring this situation into your mind's eye. Imagine you can put the situation in slow motion. Reflect on what you were doing right before the interaction, when you were on the brink of entering the scene. Freeze frame at this moment, then reflect by following the PAUSE model in the next practice. In addition to writing your reflections, you can internally visualize what could happen play by play if you were to follow the PAUSE model in this interaction. If you are feeling playful, you could divide a piece of paper into five boxes, like a cartoon, and draw what would happen for each step of PAUSE. Finally, if you are following PAUSE with other people, you can role play following PAUSE to test it out and see what you discover when you embody the model.

Having played out this situation following the PAUSE model, be aware of what is happening inside you right now. How were you impacted by picturing this way of interacting? What do you discover that might work for you?

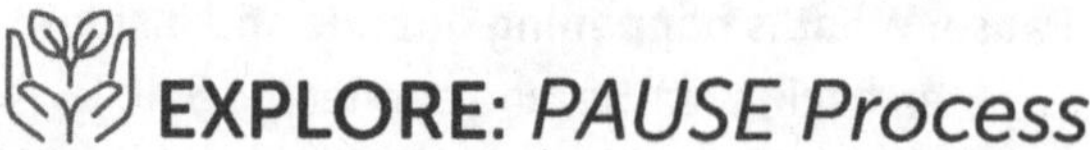

EXPLORE: *PAUSE Process*

As adults, we often feel the need to respond even when we are upset and impacted by a challenging situation. Unless someone is in danger, it generally helps to first pause, step back, and reflect before responding. Follow along with this activity to prepare for or debrief a situation or interaction.

Pause: Think of the situation or relationship that is challenging for you. What's happening outside you? (What are the circumstances? Who is there with you?) Step back for perspective. Breathe. What's happening inside you? (Notice signs of stress and Self.)

____

____

____

____

Be aware of yourself: Where are you coming from? Notice the different parts of you activated in this situation. You can list things like "A part of me thinks/feels . . ." Remembering your core Self (qualities and capacities), connect with your parts. Consider the message from these parts. What do they need?

____

____

____

____

Understand each other: Where is the other person coming from? What messages might they have? What are their needs?

____

____

____

____

Search for solutions: What needs attention? What might be possible? What is in both your power?

____

____

____

____

Experiment: What action will you try? When will you check back on the results of your action?

____

____

____

____

CHAPTER 6

In Our Power: Collaborating to Lead from Self in Schools

Pause and Reflect

- What might be possible for you, the youth you care for, and your community if you were to embrace PAUSE practices together?
- What is your role to realize this vision?
- What is in your power?

Take a moment right now to picture what might be possible as you continue to experiment with and embody the PAUSE model as a daily practice. How might you feel different on the inside? Perhaps there would be a shift in how you feel about going to work each day. When you arrive at work, imagine that you show up *differently* moment to moment—approaching the priorities of your day, listening to colleagues, offering suggestions to your administrators, attending to concerned parents, and coaching students through sticky social dynamics.

What if you invited others to join you in learning and practicing PAUSE? Envision how your students would go about their day if they had the awareness of their parts and the power to slow down and understand each other. Think about your colleagues, skillfully discussing different ideas and welcoming diverse viewpoints together. And finally, imagine that your community was empowered to access Self-leadership as a resource to fuel learning and transform collective action.

As you develop this picture in your mind, notice what stands out to you, what excites you, and what you can do. In this moment, be aware of the sensations inside you: thoughts, feelings, and physical shifts. Perhaps there are signs of hope. Now consider the implications, knowing educators around the world are by your side integrating the PAUSE model as well. A shift in education is possible with Self-leadership.

In this chapter, we will:

- Consider what is possible as we embody Self-leadership and put the PAUSE model into practice in our learning communities
- Identify what is in our power and how we can realize our vision

Essential Action for Our Children's Future

We are at a pivotal moment in the existence of humankind, facing existential challenges to the survival of future generations. The health of our planet, generational patterns of harm and injustice, and the exponential growth of technology all insist that we recognize and protect what it means to be essentially human. Confronted with these immense challenges, we may have parts that feel overwhelmed, discouraged, and alone. However, as adults charged with fostering the well-being of our children, we care for the future of our world every day. As much as our children may struggle and challenge us, we continue to see their beauty, brilliance, and essential worth. This motivates us to find a way forward, to take the next step. Together, we must carry a torch of hope and lead purposeful action.

It behooves us to embrace the task of finding what is in our power and how we can take responsibility to cultivate reconnection and collaboration—not just for our families and schools, but our wider communities and planet.

In helping us realize our innate potential, Self-leadership offers us the possibility of hope. We can feel hope when we know it is possible to access and live from our core Self, compassionately leading our parts from within. We can hold hope for our work with children because we've experienced ways to effectively relate to their parts with curiosity, guiding them to connect to their essential value and realize their potential. We can carry hope for our community, knowing that working together from Self empowers us to be harmonious, productive, and effective for the greater good.

Stories from the Field

Implementing the Self-Leadership Paradigm for Whole-School Culture

Kathryn Y. Serino, EdD, is a former superintendent of the Durham/Middlefield regional school district in Connecticut.

As a career educator and educational leader, I have always believed that individual, collective, and organizational well-being is the foundation for academic growth. Adults and children alike can persevere, problem-solve, create, and excel with a foundation of well-being.

In the process of strategic coherence planning, my administrative team and I, based on feedback from people around the district, identified three critical focus areas: student achievement, engagement, and well-being. We identified measurable outcomes and success indicators in all three areas. I felt that our first step as a district needed to be defining *well-being* as a concept. We would then identify the approach and actions to enhance, sustain, and measure well-being in our school community.

After a few staff members attended a conference and learned about the PAUSE model and how it was being used in schools, one of my administrators brought it to my attention as a promising approach to our well-being outcomes. We began training in the PAUSE model, first with a focus on teachers and other staff with the hypothesis that before adults could support students' well-being, they needed to have a deeper understanding of themselves, engage in specific practices, use the PAUSE skills, and become more Self-led.

While I understood the general design of the PAUSE model, I was not fully aware of the transformational potential until one of my teachers began using parts language to describe both personal and professional experiences. I was immediately struck by the power in this paradigm of thought and the embedded individual resourcefulness. With the PAUSE for Self-Leadership framework, adults and students alike have the necessary tools to enhance and sustain well-being and to grow personally and academically. I was also able to see this as a model that is individualized, not a boilerplate approach to social-emotional learning.

The approach in our district (which began with teachers and ultimately created school-based teacher leaders called *ambassadors*) began to have a ripple effect in terms of adults understanding themselves better and becoming more authentically forgiving of themselves and others. This deliberate grassroots effort was a transformative collaborative work in progress. Teachers who had the experience transform them and their interactions with students were now eager to share their knowledge with the entire school.

My experience of what really happened feeds my vision for what might be possible in all schools. By beginning with growing informal "leaders from the middle" who have received high quality training, there is a daily presence of people in the school practicing the PAUSE model and supporting other adults in connecting to their own Self-leadership. All adults will eventually use PAUSE language and concepts so that schools are truly invested and engaged in cultivating Self-led skills in students. Finally, the ultimate vision that could truly contribute in a definitive and measurable way is that students and all staff are engaged in knowledge, skills, and understanding that contribute to a Self-led school culture. I believe this is how small-scale, large-scale, and important changes and improvements are made in schools and—ultimately—for the greater good of the world.

What Is in Your Power?

Our hope for the future is not based on a vague, idealistic fantasy. We have the power to practice a shift in how we show up, interact, and choose action, one moment at a time. Regardless of how you are starting the work of developing Self-leadership—individually, with a small cohort of colleagues, or as a larger school community—you have the power to create meaningful change. As we approach the end of our time together in this space of learning, it's time to consider what is in your power.

Personal Exploration and Practice

This work takes hold when it arises from your own experience and convictions. Take time to reflect and recognize what ideas and practices in the PAUSE model ring true for you:

- What have you tried and experienced?
- What have been your "Aha!" moments?
- What convictions or inspirations have you discovered?

Continue to explore and sustain your own practice to embody Self-leadership as you show up each day.

Articulate Your Vision and Intention

From the vision you connected with at the beginning of this chapter, you can craft an intention statement that articulates in present tense how you practice being and how you wish to be with others and in your role. This statement will tangibly guide your everyday choices, helping you create the circumstances for the vision to become reality. Clarity of intention will help you notice when opportunities related to your vision present themselves, connect you with like-minded colleagues who hold a similar intention, and maintain patience and perseverance in the face of unexpected detours.

Take Practical Action

Too often, our plans fail because we are so inspired by a vision that we try to take on everything at once. We want to see so much change that we don't organize our efforts into practical, realistic, and measurable steps. Whether you are focused on your personal practice of the PAUSE model or ways you want to apply it in your role at school, set yourself up for success: What is one next step you can take, one time you can be with your parts, one person you can practice PAUSE with, or one way you can connect with Self in the midst of your day? Because our schools are interconnected systems, a change in *one* person or *one* area inevitably ripples throughout the community and often has much deeper impact than we appreciate. If a door opens, if an invitation is extended, or if an opportunity to share with others presents itself, say yes! If you are interested in deepening your study and integration of the PAUSE model and wish to practice in community, join us at the Self-Leadership Collaborative. We have ongoing workshops and learning spaces to nourish our global community.

Welcome All Parts

When all parts are welcome, relationships flourish and learning thrives. As you learn to detect these parts in yourself and others and understand their true intent, you defuse the tension, judgment, and conflict that blocks your ability to connect. When there is a conflict between students, see the parts at play. When preparing for a staff meeting, wonder about the parts that will be on top for your colleagues—and what they might need to feel acknowledged. When navigating dynamics between school leaders and teachers, acknowledge the different parts playing out between them and their positive intent. When listening to that upset colleague in the teachers' lounge, try welcoming their parts and see what happens. When witnessing the fluctuations of your own experience in school through the day, honor your own parts, their message, and their valuable role. By practicing the welcoming of all parts, you will shift your relationship with yourself and all those around you.

Acknowledge the Signs of Self

Seeing Self within others and in your environment supports you to connect to the state of Self within yourself. That's why continually pausing to acknowledge the signs of Self around you may be the most important step of all. When you intentionally notice the indicators of calm, curiosity, creativity, connection, compassion, clarity, confidence, and courage in your community, *being* feels safe, and your nervous system relaxes. In this secure state, you become a positive contagion, sending out signals that reverberate through the school system. Additionally, you can articulate and acknowledge the signs of Self you witness in others: name the qualities you see in a child as they are focused on a new project, thank a colleague for going above and beyond, recognize the innovation in a team project, or acknowledge others generously during staff meetings. As you highlight and celebrate Self in others, they see it too and are called into more of their full capacity. Acknowledging Self shifts our collective mindset. Simply put, Self begets Self.

Expand Collaborative Capacity

Optimize the application of the PAUSE model as you experiment with how to navigate the many interactions that fill your days. Even if you are the only person in the relationship who is familiar with PAUSE, your attunement to Self and attention to parts can influence those involved to experience a greater degree of Self-leadership. If you feel adventurous, share the PAUSE process during a team meeting or circle time with students. Let them follow the simple and intuitive steps and see what happens. Access to Self will transform your shared capacity to collaborate with and contribute to the collective.

Conclusion

Even as we strive for whole-school implementation and culture change, we can remember that the most significant changes arise from the efforts of one person at a time, one practice at a time, one word spoken at time, one choice at a time. Knowing the profound interconnection of our parts, we should not underestimate the impact of one or a few people to create a profound and sustainable system-wide shift. When we as individuals demonstrate change from the inside out, the wisdom and power of our experience attracts others. Our survival brains may cue each other's behavior, but our parts also send out a clarion call to others:

- It is possible to find relief.
- It is possible for us to work together.
- It is possible for us to heal.
- It is possible for our children to thrive.
- It is possible to nurture a more peaceful world.

Regardless of the scope of your role or your perception of your degree of influence, the most powerful way you can effect change in your school is to simply begin this work, starting with yourself from the inside out. You are more important than you know, more powerful than you believe, and more integral than can be measured. We are all a living system. It is inherently possible for us to collaborate together to lead from Self. Why not take action and discover what is possible? As we live from our power, individually and together, we nourish hope with lived experience. We see that it is possible to see our children experience joy, confidence, and connection. It is possible to discover the actions that heal our communities and uplift our planet.

Dear reader, I am grateful you have traveled this journey with me exploring the power and potential for Self-leadership in our schools. I invite you to join me as we collaborate together to lead from Self.

Invitations to Move Forward

VISUALIZE: *See Your Future*

Find a quiet place to sit. Close your eyes if you wish. Imagine that five years in the future, your longing for your school and community is now your reality. In these five years, seemingly miraculous changes have unfolded. When walking in the building, you notice the changes immediately. Visualize this future now: You are surrounded by signs and signals that your wildest dreams have come true. Interactions between adults, whether formal or informal, are different. Children love coming to school; they feel welcomed and engage wholeheartedly—they are thriving! The benefits of this transformation spread far into the community, touching the lives of thousands. Notice what you see, feel, hear, and do as you visualize your school in its ideal state. Express this vision as a drawing, a story, or simply in key words. Place this vision where you can see it, remember it, and let it evolve.

WALK: *Go in Self*

Try an experiment. When you are at work, walk through your day as if your ultimate vision is your current reality. Start with yourself. Walk through the halls, stand in conversations, sit in meetings, *as if* you are connected to Self-leadership. What do you notice? Then expand your experiment, moving through your day, as if your vision is manifesting around you. What are the signs and signals of what is already happening? What can you build on? What are the possibilities?

WRITE: *Reflect on Your Intention*

Create a mind map or list that answers these questions: "What is in my power right now to realize my vision? What are my gifts to give, my value, and my unique qualities? How do I intend to *be* amid all I *do*?" After considering these questions, distill your answers into one concise intention statement, phrased in the present tense: "I am . . ." Post this where you can remember it daily. As you remember who you are and practice Self-leadership, you will see results.

ACT: *Share Your Experience with Others*

As you recognize and experience the value of practicing the PAUSE for Self-Leadership model, share with others. Be courageous and generous to pass on possibilities for what can work to bring relief, care, and connection into your own and others' lives. Perhaps, at first, you experiment with sharing your discoveries with a friend or family members, then a colleague, then your administrator. Wonder aloud with them: How do we wish to be together? What might be possible?

Glossary of Terms and Phrases

"All parts are welcome": This core understanding in IFS supports us to remember and act from the understanding that all parts have a positive intent and naturally valuable qualities at their core.

Attend: When we attend to a part, we ask what it needs from us right now. Often a part needs one of the 4 As: acceptance, appreciation, assurance, or assistance.

Befriend: With befriending a part, we internally ask it a question to get to know its role in our inner system, its positive intent, and its story.

Blended: When we blend with a part, we merge or identify with a specific piece of our personality. We think we *are* that part, as in "I am angry" or "I am anxious."

8 Cs: These qualities often signal when we are connected to Self. The 8 Cs are calm, compassionate, courageous, curious, confident, clear, creative, and connected.

Exiles: These parts carry the negative beliefs and burdens we assumed through devaluing or traumatic experiences. As our system wants to avoid these parts at all cost, our protective parts exile them.

Firefighters: These parts serve as protectors in our inner system by reacting when exiled parts (e.g., pain, shame) are activated. Firefighters come to the rescue to douse the "flames" caused by exiles by using any strategy necessary to protect, avoid, or distract from the exile.

Managers: These parts protect us by preventing and anticipating what could activate an exile. By being and doing "good," they endeavor to keep the exile's "bad" feelings at bay.

Parts: These are the many different aspects of our personality. Parts are present at birth but evolve through our life experiences and carry our various strategies to get our needs met. Because of this, we understand they have a positive intent and cooperate as they learn to trust Self as the leader of the system.

Parts detector: When we "turn on" our parts detector, we can increase our ability to notice the different parts in ourselves and others. As we build awareness of our internal signals of thoughts, feelings, and physical sensations, we attune to the signs of our various parts.

Parts party: Certain situations can activate numerous parts of us. When too many bubble up to the surface, we may even feel flooded or confused.

Polarization: When two parts are polarized, they hold apparently opposing viewpoints, which can lead to inner confusion and even conflict. When parts unblend and allow Self to lead, the value in their perspectives can be appreciated and harmonious processes can be realized.

Protective parts: These parts protect us by keeping exiles out of sight and mind. Both firefighters and managers are protectors.

Self: Self refers to a core state of being we all possess. In this state, we are in a relaxed physiology and can access our optimal capacity for learning, connecting, and collaborating. The state of Self is often recognized and marked by the 8 Cs and 6 Ps.

Self-leadership/Self-led: When we are Self-led, we access the space of Self and consciously lead our inner system of parts and, thus, our lives.

Self-led action: This action is inspired from and reflects the qualities of Self.

Self-led listening/listening from Self: When we are Self-led, we consciously unblend from our parts so we can listen more fully from the space of Self, especially with calm, curiosity, and compassion.

Self in the system: When we access Self (and the 8 Cs), we share these qualities with all those around us, having a contagious effect and inspiring others to be more Self-led too.

6 Ps: The 6 Ps are qualities of Self that we often notice as signs of Self-led action and interaction. They are purpose, presence, perspective, persistence, playfulness, and patience.

Speak for parts: Once we are aware of our parts and their positive intent, we can represent them effectively to others by speaking *for* them (not from them), as if serving as the mediator in a conversation.

Step back: When we detect a part of us that has taken over, we can ask it to step back, or unblend. This space allows us to better understand the part and more effectively choose our action.

Unblend: When we unblend from a part, we notice it and ask it to separate from us so we can be *with* it from a place of Self.

Bibliography

Agyapong, B., Obuobi-Donkor, G., Burback, L., & Wei, Y. (2022, August 27). Stress, burnout, anxiety and depression among teachers: A scoping review. *International Journal of Environmental Research and Public Health, 19*(17), Article 10706. https://doi.org/10.3390/ijerph191710706

Alexander, R., Aragón, O. R., Bookwala, J., Cherbuin, N., Gatt, J. M., Kahrilas, I., Kästner, N., Lawrence, A., Lowe, L., Morrison, R. G., Mueller, S. C., Nusslock, R., Papadelis, C., Polnaszek, K. L., Richter, S. H., Silton, R. L., & Styliadis, C. (2021). The neuroscience of positive emotions and affect: Implications for cultivating happiness and wellbeing. *Neuroscience & Biobehavioral Reviews, 121*, 220–249. https://doi.org/10.1016/j.neubiorev.2020.12.002

American Academy of Pediatrics. (2021, October 19). *Advocacy: AAP-AACAP-CHA declaration of a national emergency in child and adolescent mental health.* https://www.aap.org/en/advocacy/child-and-adolescent-healthy-mental-development/aap-aacap-cha-declaration-of-a-national-emergency-in-child-and-adolescent-mental-health

Anderson, F. G., Sweezy, M., & Schwartz, R. C. (2017). *Internal family systems skills training manual: Trauma-informed treatment for anxiety, depression, PTSD & substance abuse.* PESI Publishing.

Benson, H. (1975). *The relaxation response.* William Morrow & Company.

Benson, H., Beary, J. F., & Carol, M. P. (1974). The relaxation response. *Psychiatry, 37*(1), 37–46. https://doi.org/10.1080/00332747.1974.11023785

Breunlin, D. C., Schwartz, R. C., & Kune-Karrer, B. M. (1992). *Metaframeworks: Transcending the models of family therapy.* Jossey-Bass.

Davidson, R. J., Kabat-Zinn, J., Schumacher, J., Rosenkranz, M., Muller, D., Santorelli, S. F., Urbanowski, F., Harrington, A., Bonus, K., & Sheridan, J. F. (2003). Alterations in brain and immune function produced by mindfulness meditation. *Psychosomatic Medicine, 65*(4), 564–570. https://doi.org/10.1097/01.psy.0000077505.67574.e3

Domitrovich, C. E., Durlak, J. A., Staley, K. C., & Weissberg, R. P. (2017). Social-emotional competence: An essential factor for promoting positive adjustment and reducing risk and school children. *Child Development, 88*(2), 408–416. https://doi.org/10.1111/cdev.12739

Durlak, J. A., Wessberg, R. P., Dymnicki, A. B., Taylor, R. D., & Schellinger, K. B. (2011). The impact of enhancing students' social and emotional learning: A meta-analysis of school-based universal interventions. *Child Development, 82*(1), 405–432. https:/doi.org/10.1111/j.1467-8624.2010.01564.x

Foundation for Self Leadership. (n.d.). https://www.foundationifs.org

Foundation for Self Leadership. (n.d.). IFS resource database. https://grantuoso.org /ifssearch

Goddard, R. (2019). *The IFS teacher manual: A training handbook for using internal family systems to improve teacher effectiveness and student success.* [ebook]. Amazon Kindle Direct Publishing.

Greenberg, M. T., Brown, J. L., & Abenavoli, R. M. (2016). *Teacher stress and health. Effects on teachers, students, and schools.* Edna Bennett Pierce Prevention Research Center, Pennsylvania State University.

Hawkes, N. (2005). *Does teaching values improve the quality of education in primary schools? A study about the impact of introducing values education in a primary school.* [Thesis]. University of Oxford.

Hawkes, N., & Hawkes, J. (2019). *The inner curriculum: How to nourish wellbeing, resilience and self-leadership.* John Catt Educational.

Herbine-Blank, T., Kerpelman, D. M., & Sweezy, M. (2015). *Intimacy from the inside out: Courage and compassion in couple therapy.* Routledge.

IFS Institute. (n.d.). https://ifs-institute.com.

IFS Institute. (n.d.). *Glossary of terms.* https://ifs-institute.com/resources/research /ifs-glossary-terms

Johnson, L. L. Adams, J., & Choi, C. (in press). Self-leadership and teacher well-being: An internal family systems approach. *International Journal of Teacher Leadership.*

Kabat-Zinn, J. (2003, June). Mindfulness-based interventions in context: past, present, and future. *Clinical Psychology: Science and Practice,* 10(2), 144–156. https://doi.org/10.1093/clipsy.bpg016

Krause, P. (2013). IFS with children and adolescents. In M. Sweezy & E. L. Ziskind (Eds.), *Internal family systems therapy: New dimensions* (pp. 35–54). Routledge.

Lovat, T., Toomey, R., Dally, K., & Clement, N. (2009): Project to test and measure the impact of values education on student effects and school ambience. [Report]. University of Newcastle, Australia.

Porges, S. W. (2007). The polyvagal perspective. *Biological Psychology, 74*(2), 116–143. https://doi.org/10.1016/j.biopsycho.2006.06.009

Rechtschaffen, D. (2014). *The way of mindful education: Cultivating well-being in teachers and students.* W. W. Norton.

Schore, A. N. (2000). *Parent-infant communication and the neurobiology of emotional development.* [Unpublished manuscript]. Department of Psychiatry and Biobehavioral Sciences, University of California at Los Angeles.

Schwartz, R. C. (2001). *Introduction to the internal family systems model.* Trailheads Publications.

Schwartz, R. C. (2008). *You are the one you've been waiting for: Bringing courageous love to intimate relationships.* Center for Self Leadership.

Schwartz, R. C. (2021). *No bad parts: Healing trauma & restoring wholeness with the internal family systems model.* Sounds True.

Schwartz, R. C., & Sweezy, M. (2020). *Internal family systems therapy* (2nd ed.). Guilford Press.

Self-Leadership Collaborative. (n.d.). https://www.selfleadershipcollaborative.com

Siegel, D. J. (2011). *The whole-brain child: 12 revolutionary strategies to nurture your child's developing mind.* Delacorte Press.

Siegel, D. J. (2014). *Brainstorm: The power and purpose of the teenage brain.* TarcherPerigee.

Siegel, D. J. (2020). *The developing mind: How relationships and the brain interact to shape who we are* (3rd ed.). Guilford Press.

Spiegel, L. (2017). *Internal family systems therapy with children.* Routledge.

U.S. Department of Education. (2021). *Supporting child and student social, emotional, behavior, and mental health needs.* https://www2.ed.gov/documents/students/supporting-child-student-social-emotional-behavioral-mental-health.pdf

van der Kolk, B. A. (2014). *The body keeps the score: Brain, mind, and body in the healing of trauma.* Viking Press.

Wells, C. (2015). Conceptualizing mindful leadership in schools: How the practice of mindfulness informs the practice of leading, *NCPEA Education Leadership Review of Doctoral Research*, 2(1), 1–23. https://files.eric.ed.gov/fulltext/EJ1105711.pdf

Willard, C. (2010). *Child's mind: Mindfulness practices to help our children be more focused, calm, and relaxed.* Parallax Press.

Acknowledgments

This model for whole-school well-being is inspired and informed by the pioneering work of Dick Schwartz, founder of Internal Family Systems (IFS)—a groundbreaking psychotherapeutic model and a transformative framework for living. I hope you have come to appreciate the simple power and unique value that IFS offers to our school communities, especially our young people. My gratitude goes to Dick Schwartz for his courage, compassion, and creativity: listening deeply to his clients, venturing into the inner space with others, and charting new pathways for us to experience our individual and collective human potential. I also want to specifically honor my teachers and mentors in the IFS model: Dr. Ralph Cohen, Ann Sinko, Rina Dubin, Ingrid Helander, and Anna Tansi, whose vision, wisdom, skill, patience, compassion, and effort have uplifted and changed the lives of thousands.

I want to acknowledge the generosity of the Foundation for Self-Leadership, the nonprofit arm of the IFS community dedicated to fostering healing and well-being through research, dissemination, and advocacy of the IFS model, especially outside the therapeutic domain. Through a generous two-year grant from the Foundation for Self-Leadership, I had the privilege of piloting this innovative approach to well-being in Connecticut schools and investing dedicated time to develop and articulate this framework. Thank you to the foundation's board, especially Executive Director Toufic Hakim, PhD, for imagining what is possible for our schools around the world and holding a steadfast commitment to endorse and support these efforts in concrete, meaningful ways. For more information on the Foundation for Self-Leadership, visit https://foundationifs.org/about.

The unique approach in this book is the fruit of a seven-year, global collaborative effort that continues to unfold. There are literally hundreds of curious, compassionate, and courageous educators from around the world who have embraced the experiment to try on a new way of understanding and connecting to themselves and others. To all in the schools where we were trusted to pilot, to all who immersed in our pioneering workshops, and to all who've ventured to embody and apply the PAUSE model in your school life and report back: Thank you! I especially want to celebrate the Global Partners and the first "Champions" cohorts, whose steady engagement has been essential in the evolution of this work. Thank you to the many who contributed to the development, review, and editing of the content of this book, especially Meera Laube-Szapiro and Erica Hermann. I want to especially thank that enthusiastic, patient, and wise Self-Leadership Collaborative core team: Joel Michor, Alexandra Barbo, Julie Faude, Kathryn Serino, Kirsten Sanderson, Melissa Zych, Heather Alexander, Jeannine O'Deens, and Amy Schaefer. And Amy—thank you for realizing the vision for the graphics in this book. What a labor of love!

Finally, I want to wholeheartedly thank my family—my parents, my husband, and my son—for your encouraging, steadfast, compassionate, and wise company on the journey of writing this book. You have not only provided very practical support (time, food, hugs, and resources), but you have graced me with the space to be on my own human journey, learning the very practices I wish to share and offer others. I am forever grateful to you!

About the Author

Photo by Andrea Kinsley

Joanna Curry-Sartori, LMFT, has over 25 years' experience counseling individuals and families and facilitating workshops and retreats for young people, parents, educators, and community leaders. Joanna's work centers on uncovering our power to be Self-led together as we respond collaboratively to the needs of our communities. After working with leadership in schools and organizations for over 15 years, Joanna recognized that many programs and initiatives that teach emotional regulation and interpersonal skills weren't addressing the root issue where people were getting stuck and what they needed to step out of fear-based self-protection and step into optimal functioning, Self-leadership. In 2011, Joanna learned about Internal Family Systems (IFS) and in it recognized not only a profound psychological model but a transformative paradigm to explain and guide productive, collaborative relationships.

In 2017, Joanna founded the Self-Leadership Collaborative (SLC) to lead the global movement to adapt and apply the essential wisdom of IFS to everyday life for people of all ages, contexts, and cultures. Initially created for educational settings, SLC programs have proven successful and adaptable for diverse environments, including corporate and nonprofit organizations.

To learn more about SLC's mission:

www.selfleadershipcollaborative.com
joanna.cs@selfleadershipcollaborative.com